GREAT CHURCHES
of LONDON

GREAT CHURCHES *of* LONDON

Derry Brabbs

FRANCES LINCOLN

CONTENTS

Introduction	6
Medieval and Tudor	8
Baroque	44
Later Georgian	126
Victorian and Edwardian	156
Twentieth Century	230
Index	268
Acknowledgements	272

HALF TITLE Union Chapel, Islington.
TITLE PAGE St Augustine's, Kilburn.
OPPOSITE St Mary Abbots, Kensington.

INTRODUCTION

Conflagration and conflict played a significant role in both the death and subsequent resurrection of many London churches. The City of London was the 'Square Mile' developed from the original Roman fortified settlement set inside the walls, and that is where the oldest City churches were located. However, the 6-m (20-ft) walls pierced by seven narrow gates created a perfectly enclosed oven for burning the City to the ground in the Great Fire of London. It took hold on the night of Sunday 2 September 1666 and raged through until Thursday. A large majority of the buildings at that time were constructed of wood, but, as such an intensive firestorm developed, even the City's stone churches were seriously affected and eighty-eight were virtually destroyed.

A young architect named Christopher Wren (1632–1723) was just thirty-three years old when his office was commissioned to build fifty-one replacement churches – and St Paul's Cathedral.

Many of those churches have survived to the present day, either unscathed or rebuilt to his original plans, having been damaged or virtually destroyed during the Blitz of 1940–1. Despite being centuries apart, those two catastrophic events resulted in significantly more than the destruction of a church's fabric, and what could not be replaced were the monuments and tombstones tracing the history of each individual church through its clergy and parishioners, be they humble or famous.

The book's first chapter dips briefly into the Medieval and Tudor period, and the star of the show is undoubtedly St Bartholomew the Great (Smithfield). The interior is pure Romanesque, the style imported by William the Conqueror and the Normans after their 1066 victory at the Battle of Hastings. Another outstanding medieval place of worship is the twelfth-century Temple Church, founded by the Knights Templar and whose circular nave is graced with effigies of the knights. The Temple Church is an excellent example of how badly damaged churches of the Second World War were so meticulously restored.

The Baroque period extended for about four decades from around 1690 and produced another architectural star in the form of Nicholas Hawksmoor (c.1661–1736). He became Wren's chief assistant and, having soaked up the genius of his master, soon evolved into a stunning architect in his own right. Fortune smiled down on him when Parliament passed a Bill in 1710 known as the 'Fifty Churches Act', designed to get Londoners back into magnificent Church of England places of worship. The Act actually only managed to finance twelve of the intended total, six of which were Hawksmoor's.

I briefly touch upon the later Georgian period (1765–1837) before arriving at the Victorian and Edwardian era up to 1918. Although the Victorians were rightly chastised for their dour approach to some churches, the early part of that era witnessed the birth of the Anglo-Catholic movement. It sought to transport church architecture back to the majestic Gothic period and the captivating religious theatre of High Mass.

The final chapter looks at some of London's twentieth-century churches, an architectural portfolio of quite fascinating buildings representing a variety of Christian faiths.

London is privileged to have such an impressive collection of churches but, just like our own bodies, not all are fighting fit. Were it not for English Heritage, other sources of funding and the many millions donated by the National Lottery Fund, London could be deprived of some of its priceless religious treasures.

Chancel arch of London Oratory.

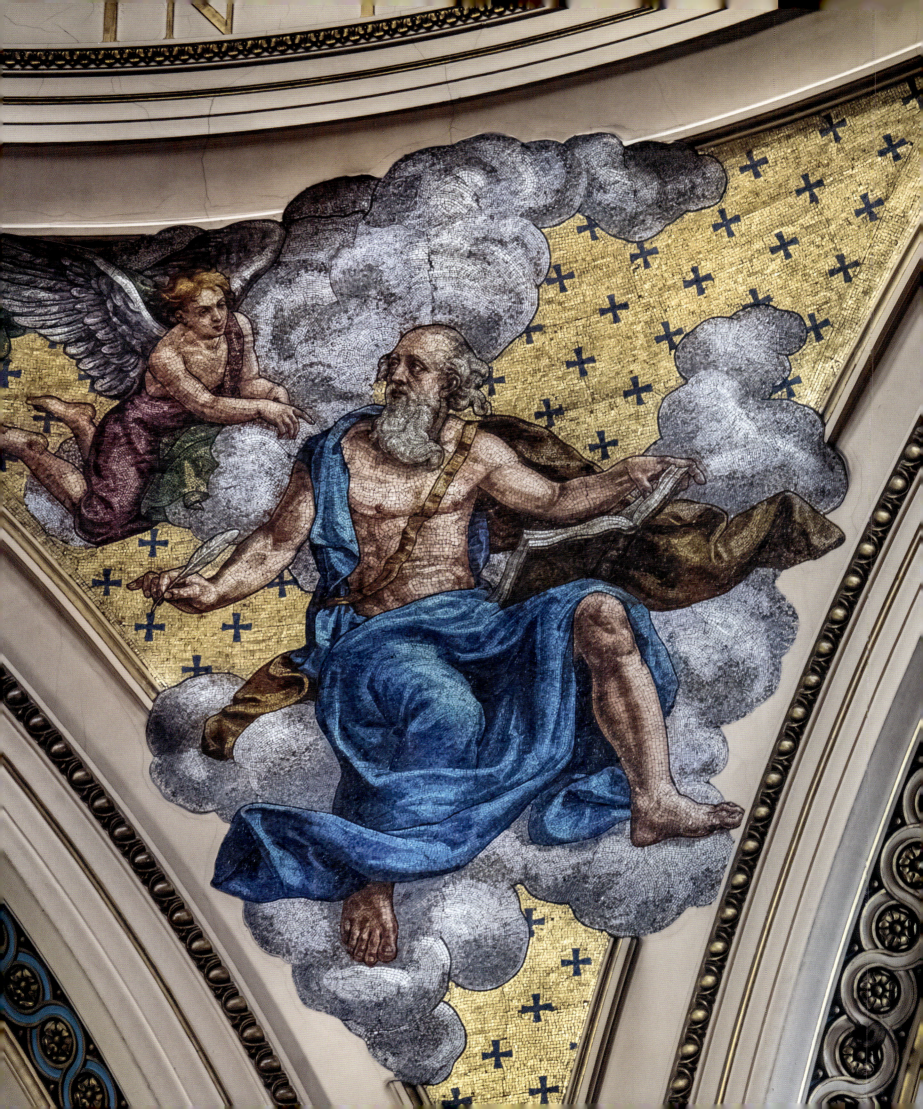

MEDIEVAL AND TUDOR

St Bartholomew the Great

WEST SMITHFIELD, EC1

St Bartholomew the Great was founded in 1123 by Rahere, a respected and much liked courtier to King Henry I (r. 1100–35), following his survival from a life-threatening illness while on a pilgrimage to Rome. As he lay being lovingly cared for in the Italian hospital, Rahere mused that he might well have just died had the same circumstances afflicted him in London. Those thoughts were amplified by a dramatic vision experienced on returning home, a dream in which the Apostle, St Bartholomew, showed him whereabouts in London he should establish the church. Rahere did exactly that after seeking help from the king, and the timing of his request could not have come at a more beneficial time. Henry's life had just been cruelly transformed by the death of William, his son and heir, in the catastrophic *White Ship* disaster off the coast of Normandy in 1120. Scores of Henry's close friends and advisors also perished, so when Rahere stated that he wished to build the Augustinian priory and church, plus a nearby hospital for the poor, the king made generous donations of funding, endowments and parcels of land.

The most immediate visual landmark is the extended façade of Smithfield Meat Market, but the church of St Bartholomew is not readily visible. However, sandwiched between two modern buildings in West Smithfield stands the original thirteenth-century doorway, surmounted by a black and white half-timbered Elizabethan dwelling. Although this now leads through into the open churchyard, it was originally the entrance to the priory church's nave, most of which was demolished in 1539 at the Dissolution. The current church doorway opens into the one surviving bay of the nave leading into the choir and transepts that had been allowed to survive and continue as a parish church after the Dissolution. It is at this moment that visitors are suddenly transported back to the Romanesque style of architecture introduced by the Normans. The heavy solemnity of the massive arches and pillars combines with the natural darkness of the ambulatories and interior to create a monumental and timeless atmosphere. This Romanesque gem is the oldest parish church in London, and although some did date back to that same architectural period, none survived both the 1666 Great Fire of London and the Blitz of the Second World War.

St Bartholomew's had its red brick tower added during the third decade of the seventeenth century, but thereafter, architectural maintenance gradually diminished. There were partial restoration attempts towards the end of the eighteenth century, but the church fell into a deplorable state as significant parts of it were taken for secular use. It was patently deemed that parishioners needed little more than a font, altar, pulpit and pews. So the cloisters became horse stables, the north transept a blacksmith's shop, a school was established in the upper gallery, and the Lady Chapel housed three tenements and also became a printing shop in which Benjamin Franklin served as an apprentice in 1725–6. That was later replaced by a fringe-making factory, and all those small industries gradually eroded the fabric and structure of the church.

The approach to St Bartholomew the Great is through an archway from Smithfield and then along a path across the current churchyard that originally housed the nave before it was demolished in the mid-sixteenth century as a result of Henry VIII's Dissolution of the Monasteries.
PREVIOUS PAGES St Bartholomew the Great.

It was not until 1885 that the commission for restoring the church was given to the architect Aston Webb (1849–1930), whose brother was a churchwarden at St Bartholomew's. That might explain why an architect renowned for projects such as Buckingham Palace, the Mall's Admiralty Arch and the Natural History Museum may have been tempted to undertake the restoration of that ailing church. It was a challenge continued until completion of the cloister's east walk that was officially opened by Princess Mary (daughter of King George V) in 1928, just two years prior to Webb's death.

St Bartholomew's benefited financially from the Charter granted by Henry I for the hosting of a three-day that commenced on 24 August, the Feast Day of St Bartholomew. What originally took place on the vast grassy area just outside the City walls known as 'Smoothfield' was more or less a textile market. However, it gradually escalated from that trade event called the Cloth Fair, into a festivity that extended up to fourteen days during certain eras and comprised numerous sideshows, stage entertainments and alcohol-fuelled debauchery. It was the latter element that made the Victorian authorities force its closure in 1855. Nevertheless, during the centuries through which it had thrived, the Fair had helped fund the Augustinian Priory, St Bartholomew's Hospital and also its own church, St Bartholomew the Less, that had been built within the hospital grounds.

OPPOSITE The view from the altar and sanctuary towards the choir highlights just how solid the Romanesque style of church architecture introduced by the Normans actually was. There are some minimal decorations around the arches but these churches were just so incredibly imposing.

ABOVE The oriel window was added by Prior William Bolton around 1517 to light his private chapel and lodgings, but also to ensure that he had a view down into the church. The symbol directly below the glass shows a crossbow bolt piercing a wine barrel.

14 GREAT CHURCHES OF LONDON

ABOVE The east walk of the cloister was not finally acquired and perfectly renovated until 1928, and its access point is close by the last section of the original nave. It is a most atmospheric place and is now used for receptions, banquets and other special occasions.

OPPOSITE: Ancient and modern pieces of St Bartholomew's sculpture. TOP LEFT *The Risen Christ* by Josefina De Vasconcellos (1904–2005). TOP RIGHT The Perpendicular period tomb of Rahere, St Bart's founder, lies in the chancel. BOTTOM RIGHT Virgin and Child. BOTTOM LEFT *Exquisite Pain* is Damien Hirst's statue of St Bartholomew after being skinned alive.

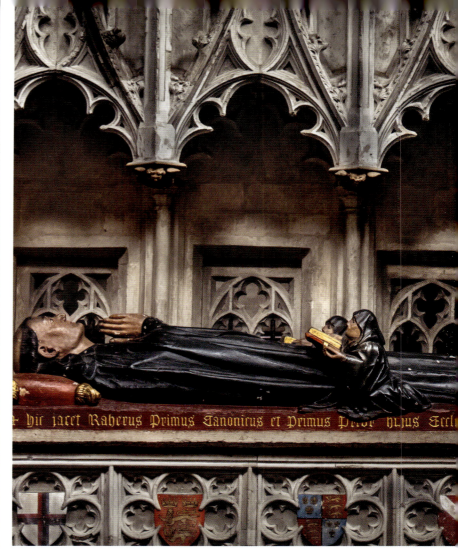

The Temple Church

TEMPLE, EC4

A distinctive black and white half-timbered building on Fleet Street is pierced by an ancient gated archway and a passageway, then leads down into the maze of barristers' chambers set in the tranquillity of the Temple. Two of the City's four Inns of Court, the Inner and Middle Temples, occupy that piece of land leading down to the River Thames, and set in the heart of it is the Temple Church. This captivating building was founded by the Knights Templar in the twelfth century and modelled on the circular church of the Holy Sepulchre in Jerusalem that was built over the empty grave of the Risen Jesus. The Templars were founded to protect pilgrims travelling across Europe to the Holy Land following the Crusaders' victory in the First Crusade (1096–99).

The Temple Church was in use by 1163 and formally consecrated by Heraclius, Patriarch of Jerusalem, in 1185. Architecturally, the whole interior was built using designs from the Gothic period rather than the previous Romanesque style, which therefore makes the Temple Church one of the earliest in England from that architectural era. The width of the circular nave is 59ft (18m), and six grouped Purbeck marble piers form a broad, rib-vaulted ambulatory, above which is a triforium and, finally, a clerestory with slim, round-headed windows. It is well worth making the climb up a flight of stairs to the triforium as much of the floor is covered with a collection of Victorian tiles on which graphic designs are interspersed with horse-riding Templars and mythical creatures. The circular interior wall of the nave is lined with low blind arcading, interspersed with many grotesque sculptures of the kind one usually sees on the outside of a church from this period.

Although there had been an earlier chancel, the one that now stretches away from the circular nave was begun in the thirteenth century during the reign of Henry III (r. 1216–72). The current chancel is a perfect complement to the atmospheric nave and comprises three aisles of equal height supported by slender marble columns and evenly illuminated by deep, triple lancet windows. This serious upgrade in architectural style was due largely to the king himself who, having attended the consecration in 1240, was so captivated by the legends of the Templars that he proclaimed that both he and the queen wanted to be buried there. Henry did finally opt for Westminster Abbey, but his dreams nevertheless generated a superb piece of architecture. The reredos behind the altar was a later addition made in 1682–3 by William Rounthwaite, a member of Christopher Wren's team who also refitted the interior. The east end is completed by the triple window designed by Carl Edwards (1914–85) and installed in 1957–8. It is acknowledged as being some of the finest post-war glass in London, being intricate, delicate and with deep, rich tones; his technique involved using pieces of medieval glass and was therefore difficult to replicate.

By 1291, the Templars had lost their last base in the Holy Land, were eventually suppressed in 1312, and

---

Tucked away between Fleet Street and the Thames is the labyrinth of lanes and passageways of the Inner and Middle Temples. In its very heart lies the Temple Church, built for the Knights Templar and consecrated in 1185 by the Patriarch of Jerusalem.

THE TEMPLE CHURCH 19

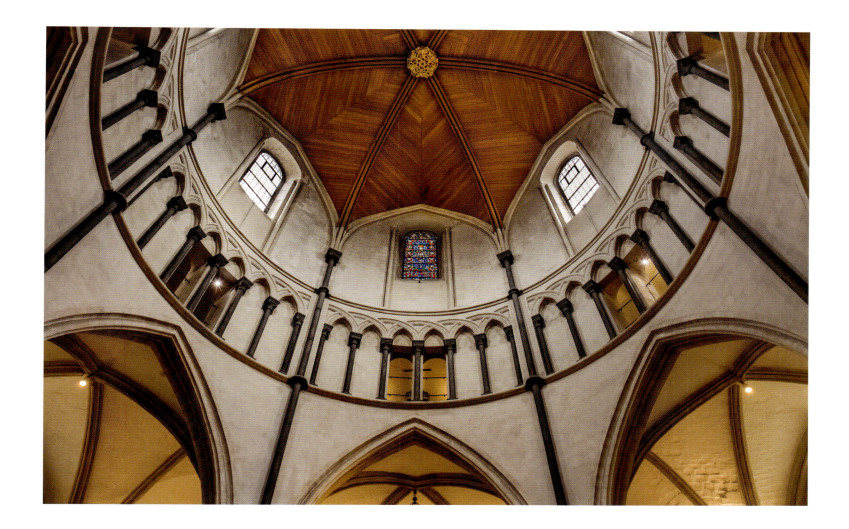

their properties handed to a similar Order, the Knights Hospitaller of St John. In hindsight, it was agreed that their demise was largely instigated by King Philip of France. He was deep in debt and wanted access to the wealth and lands accumulated within the Templar organization, so most of the charges actually levelled again them were simply untrue. After the sixteenth-century Reformation under Henry VIII, the Temple Church passed to the Crown and enjoys the status of Royal Peculiar, a title making it answerable to the Crown rather than to Bishops and Church authorities. In 1608 King James I gave the Temple to the two Inns on condition that they used it for the education of lawyers and ensured it was always well maintained.

When the Temple suffered serious damage from fire caused by incendiary bombs dropped during the Blitz of 1941, the round nave suffered more than the chancel, and much blazing debris tumbled down onto the effigies of the medieval knights laid out on the floor. It was a glorious twist of fate that several of the knights had been reproduced in plaster casts almost a century earlier to be exhibited at the Great Exhibition of 1851. These medieval knight effigies have always fascinated visitors, and numbers escalated dramatically when American author Dan Brown published his *Da Vinci Code* novel in 2003, and Tom Hanks starred in the film version three years later, featuring scenes shot in the Temple Church.

OPPOSITE: TOP LEFT The church's Romanesque-style main portal was created during the twelfth century. TOP RIGHT View from the circular nave down the chancel. BOTTOM LEFT Gilbert Marshall, 4th Earl of Pembroke. BOTTOM RIGHT The triforium's floor is covered with a visually stunning collection of Victorian tiles.

ABOVE The circular nave comprises six piers whose arches lead up to the triforium. The use of dark Purbeck marble is a stroke of architectural genius, because if it had all been pale stone, there would not be this graphic outline of the nave's beautiful symmetry.

20 GREAT CHURCHES OF LONDON

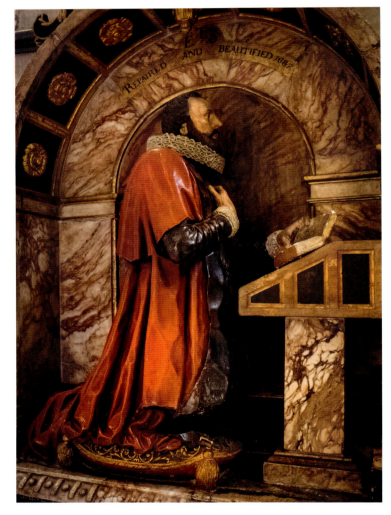

ABOVE LEFT Sir Edward Plowden (d. 1584), who was actually a Catholic and treasurer of the Middle Temple. His epitaph reads 'I have lived in a dangerous channel, I die in harbour'. ABOVE RIGHT Richard Martin (d. 1618) loved parties and his tomb bears the inscription 'Repaired and Beautified'.

OPPOSITE The chancel's triple east window was the work of Carl Edwards and donated by the Glaziers Company as part of the post-war restoration project. The left and right panels depict the Templars and important monarchs, with the central window focusing on the Life of Christ.

St Etheldreda's

ELY PLACE, EC1

St Etheldreda's lies in the cul-de-sac of Ely Place, close to the western end of Smithfield Market. The name of the street was derived from its close links with the Cambridgeshire cathedral city of Ely and St Etheldreda. She was the daughter of an East Anglian king born around 630 CE, twice married (first husband died) but then retired to a nunnery in 672 CE. The following year she founded a double monastery for monks and nuns on the site that was later occupied by Ely Cathedral.

Etheldreda died in 679 from a tumour in her neck. Sixteen years later, her sister requested that the tomb be opened and it revealed that her body was untainted and the tumour perfectly healed. Etheldreda's shrine thereafter became a much visited pilgrimage destination, but of course was ultimately destroyed during the mid-sixteenth-century Dissolution ordered by Henry VIII.

The land occupied by St Etheldreda's was acquired from St Paul's Cathedral in the mid-thirteenth century by the Bishop of Ely, and the chapel thereafter served the Palace of the Bishops of Ely, also erected on that site. It was a most lavish place set amid acres of extensive gardens, orchards and agricultural land, a practice that became quite common from the thirteenth century onwards. As many members of the nation's religious hierarchy frequently had to be engaged in parliamentary matters, or had been appointed to high-ranking civil offices, having secondary country estates within easy reach of the capital seemed quite sensible.

However, their history was far from straightforward and both the palace and chapel had mixed legacies in terms of ownership and faith. One of the most significant periods was during the reign of Queen Elizabeth I, who, for a period, had been closely associated with Sir Christopher Hatton and in 1578 formally granted him the Bishop of Ely's Palace. The bishops were outraged at this act of 'property piracy', but it transpired that Hatton was actually more interested in developing the extensive gardens. That connection resulted in the naming of the road in what is now the heart of the world-famous diamond district, and Hatton Garden runs parallel to Ely Place. The palace was let to the Spanish ambassador in the seventeenth century, and during that period, St Etheldreda's chapel was transformed for legally permitted Catholic use. The church was on the verge of being consumed during the Great Fire of 1666, but nature intervened and winds swept the flames well away from Ely Place.

During the following century, the palace was demolished for housing development and the chapel remained in use by a variety of religious groups. It was in 1874 that the church was actually purchased at auction by the Catholic Rosminian Order of Charity, and it remains in their care as a Catholic parish church. St Etheldreda's east front is the only visible exterior part of the church, as it is tightly set between buildings on either side. Entry is down a flight of steps and one then walks along a passageway leading towards the main body of the church. Halfway along, a flight of steps descends into the thirteenth-century crypt, a meticulously restored and

Ely Place in Holborn is a private street, but St Etheldreda's is clearly signposted on the gatehouse for visitors and worshippers. The church was once a chapel to the medieval Palace of the Bishops of Ely, and is now all that survives from that era.

24 GREAT CHURCHES OF LONDON

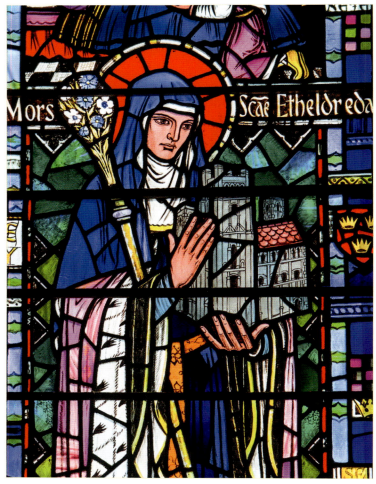

atmospheric space that served as a bomb shelter for the local community during the Second World War. Leading on from the crypt, the passageway arrives at a substantial flight of stairs leading up to the aisleless upper church. The symmetry and atmosphere of this intimate space is truly mesmerizing and one's eyes are hypnotically drawn to the stained glass window that almost fills the east end. This was designed and created by Edward Nuttgens, who was born in Germany at the end of the nineteenth century but spent most of his life studying and working in England. The window has all the ingredients of a medieval glass, but the design and portrayal of the figures has the aura of the Arts & Crafts movement. In total contrast, the west window by Charles Blakeman dates from 1964 and is dedicated to the English Martyrs who were persecuted and executed for their Catholic faith during the Reformation.

The Martyrs are also represented by the almost full-size statues created by May Blakeman during the 1960s and set on the walls in between the arches. St Etheldreda's may not necessarily be a unique survivor of the old two-storey style of church architecture but, in the context of London churches, it truly is a treasure that should be visited and admired.

ABOVE LEFT The Catholic Martyrs persecuted during the Reformation are represented by almost full-size statues created by May Blakeman during the 1960s and set on the walls in between the arches. ABOVE RIGHT A portrayal of St Etheldreda holding her church on a segment of the east window.

OPPOSITE The aisle-free main body of St Etheldreda's with its vast east window, graphically stepped altar, atmospheric lighting and the almost life-like Catholic Martyrs creates a really intimate and most moving atmosphere. OVERLEAF Centre panels of the east window.

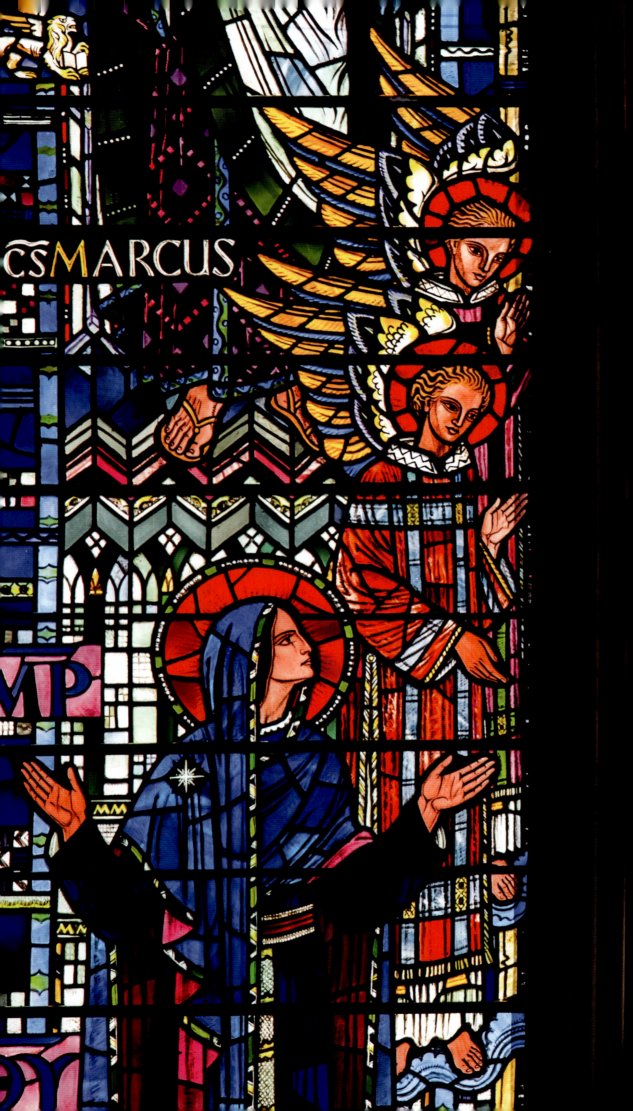

28 GREAT CHURCHES OF LONDON

ABOVE The thirteenth-century crypt of St Etheldreda's is an evocative corner of medieval London, especially when devoid of the furniture used for weddings and other social gatherings. Such twin-level churches are not very common and the nave/crypt combination is a truly wonderful place.

OPPOSITE: TOP LEFT Virgin and Child statue set in the crypt. TOP RIGHT Coat of arms dating back to the reign of Charles I. BOTTOM LEFT Detail of pillars and arch into the nave. BOTTOM RIGHT Steps leading up into the church from the main corridor.

All Hallows by the Tower

BYWARD STREET, EC3

All Hallows by the Tower is the City's oldest church and used to be called All Hallows Barking. That original version referred to its seventh-century origin as a chapel for Barking Abbey, located some 13 km (8 miles) further east from the City. The abbey was founded by Erkenwald, who also served as Bishop of London from 675–93 CE. All Hallows stands on raised ground overlooking the Tower of London and it is extraordinary to think that the original church was already 300 years old when its neighbour started to be built. The Norman church that succeeded the Saxon building was constructed towards the end of the eleventh century after William the Conqueror had completed the monumental White Tower. However, All Hallows did later discover that one of the downsides of its proximity to the Tower of London was its obligation to receive and temporarily bury a significant number of headless 'traitors' after execution.

All Hallows was lucky to have survived a huge explosion in 1649 when barrels of gunpowder in a nearby chandler's yard caught fire and exploded, causing cataclysmic damage and many deaths. The church had its windows blown out and the tower was so badly damaged that it had to be rebuilt. As the tower was entering its final phase of construction, the 1666 Great Fire of London rampaged through the City of London in the direction of All Hallows. The famous diarist, Samuel Pepys, lived close by in Seething Lane and was able to climb to the top of the new tower to observe the advancing flames. However, while he was watching and writing notes for his diary, his next door neighbour Admiral William Penn (father of William Penn, founder of Pennsylvania) was able to get his men from the nearby naval shipyard to blow up houses set between the church and rapidly approaching fire storm, thereby depriving the advancing flames of further fuel.

Just over two and a half centuries later, All Hallows suffered the same fate as many other City churches when they were either severely damaged or totally destroyed during the Blitz of 1940–1. There were two aerial attacks in which bombs smashed through the roof, the ruins of which cascaded down onto the floor, destroying furnishings, memorials and other treasures. The damage must have been drastic and heartbreaking but, unlike most bombed City churches, All Hallows was blessed with monumental strokes of good fortune. Despite the massive structural damage, several important memorials and furnishings survived, one of the most treasured being an intricately carved font cover created by Grinling Gibbons in 1682 that was fortuitously hidden elsewhere. The exploding munitions and falling rubble penetrated the church floor and revealed treasures from past eras that are now viewable by visitors. Perhaps the most striking is a Saxon arch that had remained hidden for centuries until its plaster and brickwork frontage was shaken free by the explosions. The entire crumbled masonry and timber jigsaw was then successfully tackled by the architectural partnership of Lord Mottistone and Paul Paget. They extended the undercroft and that is now a fascinating museum housing a Roman tessellated pavement, fragments

---

All Hallows by the Tower enjoys an elevated position overlooking the Tower of London and River Thames. After many years of having the sky to itself, the elegant copper-clad spire now creates a visually agreeable partnership with its modern neighbour, the Sky Garden.

32 Great Churches of London

ALL HALLOWS BY THE TOWER 33

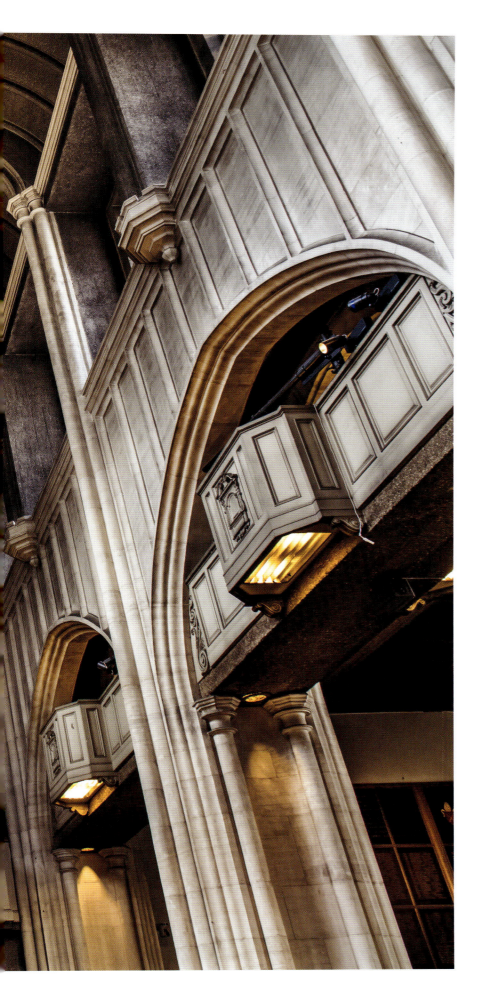

from three Saxon crosses, tiny chapels and other items from many periods. They gave the church a fresh feeling rather than delving back centuries to recreate one particular phase of the Gothic architectural styles, although some of their work has elements of the Perpendicular. Much of the stonework used for the nave's pillars and arches was subtly coloured and textured Cotswold limestone.

The walls, floor and windows are enriched by a collection of statues, monuments and glass. Set on the nave floor is an effigy of the Reverend 'Tubby' Clayton, vicar of All Hallows for forty years from 1922–62, who was also the founder of TocH (army signaller's jargon for Talbot House). It was originally established near Ypres in Belgium as a temporary haven for First World War soldiers, and still functions as a humanitarian community in conjunction with the All Hallows Trust set up in 1927.

Many London churches are hemmed in, but at the time of its reconstruction, All Hallows was in an open space due to the destruction of surrounding buildings that had not been rebuilt. Its elevated position was significantly enhanced when Lord Mottistone added a Scandinavian-style spire of Columbian pine sheathed in copper onto the existing brick tower. The restoration work began in 1948 and All Hallows was rededicated in 1957, in the presence of Her Majesty Queen Elizabeth the Queen Mother.

All Hallows survived the Great Fire of London but fared less well during the Second World War, sustaining substantial bomb damage. The elegant rebuilding bears hints of an interpretation of the Perpendicular style, with very clean cut and slightly textured stone. The first organ was installed in 1520 and the latest was the post-war instrument of 1957. Below the organ sits the Stuart Royal Arms of the 1660 Restoration of Charles II to the throne.

All Hallows by the Tower

OPPOSITE The Lady Chapel houses the Croke monument dedicated to Alderman John Croke (d. 1477). It was shattered into 150 fragments by a bomb blast but was pieced back together. Standing on the memorial is a casket containing the TocH lamp, donated by Edward, Prince of Wales in 1922.

ABOVE Many ancient treasures are portrayed down in the Crypt Museum and one of my favourites is the Peacock Pluteus Stone. It depicts two peacocks drinking from the Fountain of Life and is apparently very similar to one discovered in a tenth-century Veneto island church.

36 GREAT CHURCHES OF LONDON

ABOVE The main altar lies directly below the vast east window and a dramatic mural depicting the Last Supper by artist Brian Thomas OBE (1912–89). Because the figure of Christ dominates the centre, the altar is not furnished with the customary central cross.

OPPOSITE The All Hallows original pulpit was destroyed in the Second World War, and its seventeenth-century replacement carved in the style of Grinling Gibbons comes from another church that was destroyed and not rebuilt. The tester replicates the scallop shells associated with the Santiago de Compostela pilgrimage.

St Katharine Cree

LEADENHALL STREET, EC3

St Katharine Cree is set on Leadenhall Street not far from Aldgate, the most easterly of the City's original seven gates. The first church on this site was built towards the end of the thirteenth century. It was erected in a corner of the cemetery serving the Augustinian priory of Holy Trinity, whose prior decided that his canons were not sufficiently respected by the local population during Mass and that more silence was required. The church's condition declined over time and was rebuilt at the end of the fifteenth century, but sadly did not survive for many decades because its association with the priory resulted in almost total demolition during Henry VIII's Dissolution of the Monasteries (1536–41).

The church lay in that ruinous state for years until the parishioners finally decided to rebuild it in 1628. The only surviving part of its predecessor was a portion of the tower dating back to 1504, and the church's reconstruction took place in a most interesting architectural period when church building had significantly declined. Although its exterior is relatively plain in appearance, the interior of St Katharine's is a fascinating combination of Gothic and Classical styles.

The actual layout is conventional, comprising six-bay arcades and aisles of Corinthian columns with coffered round arches that run the full length of the church.

Above the arches the style reverts to a Gothic clerestory, and both the nave and aisles have shallow plaster rib vaults. One of the most aesthetically pleasing aspects of the interior is the soft blue of the arches and vaults, creating a geometric design leading one's eye down to the magnificent east end. Above the altar is a large circular window set in a square frame, and because St Katharine's escaped both the 1666 Fire of London and the Blitz, it is still filled with much of its original seventeenth-century glass. The main window is thought to represent the saint to whom the church is dedicated, and St Katharine (also spelt with a 'C') was martyred for her devout Christianity in the fourth century by Roman Emperor Maxentius. She was to be tortured and executed on a spiked wheel but it simply fragmented when Katharine touched it and she was subsequently beheaded. The popular Catherine Wheel firework derives its name from the martyred saint.

In the south-east corner of the church is the Laud Chapel, established by the Society of King Charles the Martyr in 1960. It is dedicated to William Laud, who had consecrated the rebuilt church in 1631 and was appointed Archbishop of Canterbury in 1633 by King Charles I. It is thought that the king favoured Laud because they jointly agreed on a revised version of religion that started to take the English Church back to its Catholic pre-Reformation days. Not everybody in the higher echelons of government and religion shared those views, and in 1645 Archbishop Laud was executed in the Tower of London. Records show that he was one of those whose headless corpse spent time in All Hallows by the Tower before being delivered to its final resting place at St John's College, Oxford. Despite its location amid the areas of massive development in the City, St Katharine's nevertheless

St Katharine Cree fortunately stood beyond the eastern limits of the Great Fire. The main body of the current church from 1630 was built onto the surviving tower of 1504. The elegant cupola was added in 1776 and offers a good visual contrast with 30 St Mary Axe, also known as The Gherkin.

40 GREAT CHURCHES OF LONDON

retains a portion of the churchyard that was an integral part of its history, and this small garden has just a few stone remnants from that era. The church interior is adorned with memorials spanning several centuries, including a significant one dedicated to Sir Nicholas Throckmorton (c.1515–71), whose recumbent effigy lies on a bed supported by Tuscan columns. This memorial joins the tower in having been from the previous church. Perhaps the most intriguing memorial is the mid-seventeenth-century font donated by Sir John Gayer, a merchant and Lord Mayor of London in 1646. While travelling through Syria, he encountered a lion and, in fear of his life, prayed to God for salvation. The lion duly moved away and, upon his safe return home, Sir John presented the font and made significant endowments to charity. There was one condition attached, namely that a 'Lion Sermon' should be held every October, and that request has been honoured by the church every single year up to the present day. Because the church does not have an actual parish, in 1952 it was designated a Guild Church by the Bishop of London to offer support and guidance to City workers, and St Katharine's has become a much valued member of that community.

St Katharine's interior is one of the most visually interesting churches of the Jacobean period, a time when church building was at a significantly reduced rate, and the few English churches built in the pre-Civil War period tended to cite St Katharine's as their architectural reference.

ST KATHARINE CREE 41

ST KATHARINE CREE 43

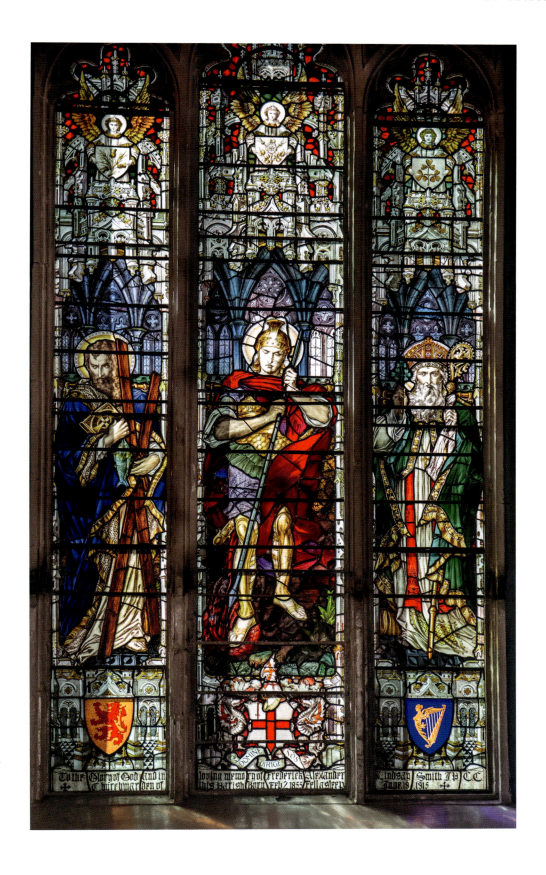

OPPOSITE: TOP LEFT The circular east window representing the wheel upon which St Katharine was to be executed. TOP RIGHT A 1964 wood sculpture of King Charles by the Society of King Charles the Martyr. BOTTOM The ceiling bosses display the arms of City livery companies.

ABOVE The 'Lost Window' set in the south aisle was reinstalled in 2018 after detective work and reconstruction following the removal and reassembly of glass fragments from a Second World War damaged window. It took a full five years to complete that amazing task.

BAROQUE

St Magnus the Martyr

LOWER THAMES STREET, EC3

St Magnus the Martyr was built on the northern bank of the River Thames. It stands close by the crossing point of the original stone-built London Bridge, opened in 1209 and not replaced until 1831. There have been debates about which of the several martyrs of that name was actually being honoured, and the eventual outcome was Magnus, the Norwegian Earl of Orkney, who was killed in *c*.1117 and canonized in 1135. The old London Bridge actually developed into a 'high street' with houses, shops and taverns lining both sides. There were huge areas of trade and activity on either side of the bridge's northern end, and it was also where the famous Billingsgate Fish Market developed – all combining to create a significant parish and congregation for the church. A detailed and informative model of that old London Bridge is on display inside the church. The buildings were all removed in 1760–1 to enable greater room for pedestrians and horse-drawn traffic to safely cross the Thames. St Magnus's then had to have its original west bay demolished to create an archway under the tower for a new pathway to the bridge.

Its aesthetically perfect setting made it a prominent element of many paintings and, ironically, the only other structure soaring above the London skyline was the Monument. Those including that memorial to the Great Fire of London in their composition may not have realized that both were actually the work of Sir Christopher Wren, who devoted so much time to restoring London after the fire. Wren rebuilt the body of the church between 1671–6 and returned to start work on the steeple in 1703. It is 56m (184ft) high and comprises a short spire sitting on a lead dome, which then rests upon an octagonal lantern.

St Magnus the Martyr is a church of elegance and atmosphere that starts with the twin staircases curving upwards from the main entrance to the organ gallery. The organ was built by Abraham Jordan and his son and theirs was the first to have a foot-operated swell box that fluctuates the volume. Inside the nave, Wren's layout is enhanced by the significant amounts of light flooding in through the south windows and clerestory, making the gilded tunnel vault and fluted Ionic columns positively shimmer. One of the most visually appealing aspects is that there are no heavy pews, and the skeletal ones now in place are angled in such a way that all members of the congregation are slightly more connected and not simply staring straight ahead. That layout also draws everyone into being able to automatically focus on both the high altar and elegant carved small pulpit with a really large sounding board.

The church underwent a significant restoration by Martin Travers in the early 1920s, both adding to, and transforming, the existing layout to create a significant Anglo-Catholic church. He added a top tier to Wren's already splendid reredos, surmounted on each corner by golden angels and then a rood group sits high above in the centre. The Lady Altar stands in the north-east corner and its reredos was created with an

---

The reredos was restored by Martin Travers in 1924 and includes an eye-catching trio of Moses and Aaron painted on either side of the altar and directly above the sculpted gold 'Pelican in Her Piety', an early Christian symbol of self-sacrifice. PREVIOUS PAGES St Mary Aldermary.

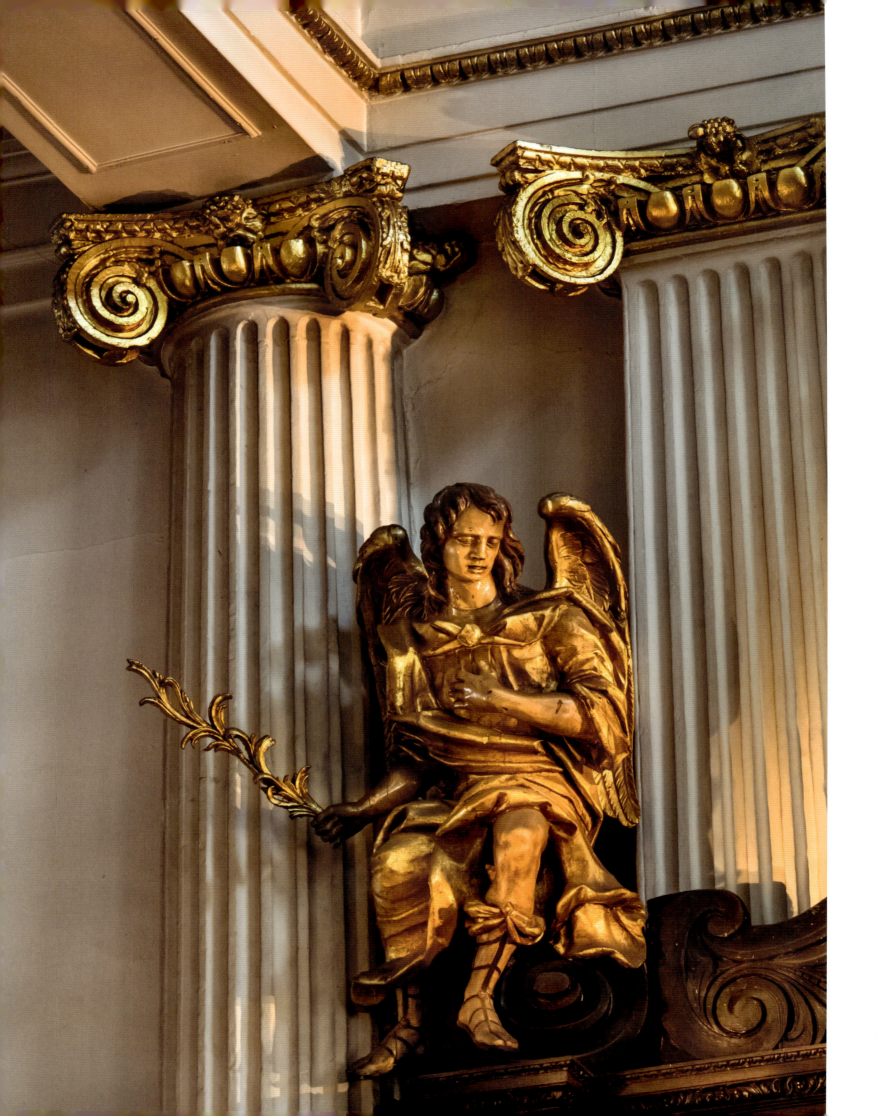

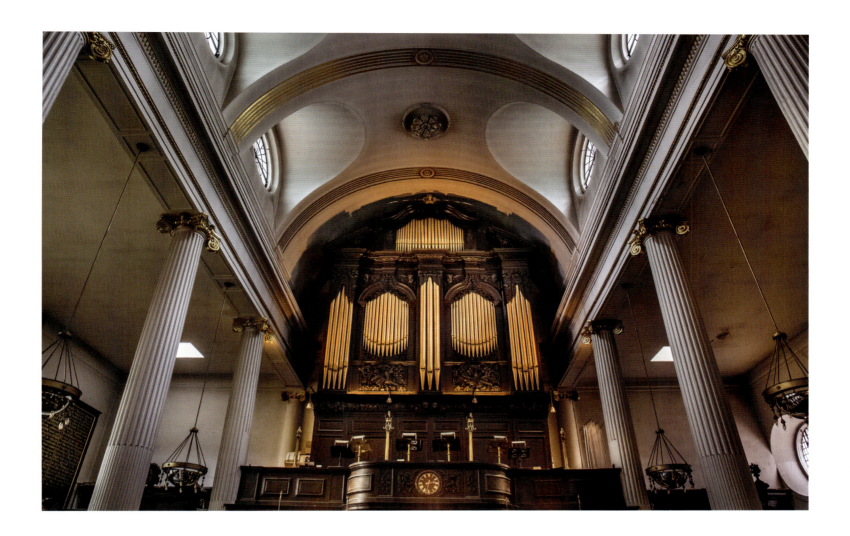

imposing recycled door from the Wren era. It is approached past a statue of the Virgin and Child that is an almost perfect replica of the one in the Catholic pilgrimage church of Our Lady of Walsingham in Norfolk. Travers' work was directed by Father Fynes-Clinton who served as rector from 1921 until his death in 1959. He had also accentuated his devotion to the Anglo-Catholic Church by refounding the Fraternity of Our Lady de Salve Regina that originated in 1343 but had remained disbanded since the Reformation.

The south-east corner also has an altar whose reredos was originally the extravagant door case for the south-east entrance. This altar was erected in 1951 to serve as a lasting memory to the dead of both world wars. The high altar is encircled by the original wrought iron altar rails and, despite all the restorations and repairs carried out over many centuries, the undulating stone flooring dotted with memorial stones remains largely untouched.

The north wall of the nave has been cleverly redesigned with small round windows to minimize the effect of traffic noise as St Magnus the Martyr sits just a pavement's width from the dual carriageway 'racetrack' of Lower Thames Street. Aesthetically, it is sadly also hemmed in by two vast office blocks but, even so, none of those negative elements will ever affect the atmosphere and artistic beauty of the church.

OPPOSITE The angels set either side of the main altar's reredos were part of the 1920s restoration, and the original columns with gold embellishment were mentioned in T.S. Eliot's famous poem, 'The Waste Land', 'where the walls of Magnus Martyr hold inexplicable splendour of white and gold'.

ABOVE The west end of the nave is dominated by the gallery and a visually striking organ, equipped with a double-storey array of pipes reaching up to the roof. The decorative carving on the organ's façade represents one of the finest examples of that genre in any London church.

50 Great Churches of London

ABOVE LEFT At the end of the south aisle and set in a reredos, originally part of the church entrance, is the Chapel of Christ the King. That artistically unusual portrayal of Jesus Christ was actually based upon an element of Van Eyck's fifteenth-century altar piece in Belgium's Ghent Cathedral.

ABOVE RIGHT AND OPPOSITE The Lady Chapel is located at the northeast end and not in an enclosed part of the church. Just before reaching the altar, worshippers will pass the beautiful replica statue of Our Lady of Walsingham, the famous pilgrimage site set in rural Norfolk that has both Catholic and Anglican shrines.

St Stephen Walbrook

WALBROOK, EC4

St Stephen Walbrook derives its name from the river that once flowed through this part of the City. The first church was thought to have stood on the east bank and the earliest written record of its existence was during the reign of William the Conqueror. St Stephen's was later rebuilt in the first half of the fifteenth century but subsequently destroyed by the Great Fire of 1666.

As this was Christopher Wren's parish church, he made it a priority in the post-fire rebuilding process, with design and construction of the main body taking place between 1672–80. Constriction of available space had enforced a rather plain stone rectangle and tower, but Wren returned in 1713 to create one of his more ornate spires to light up the rather dull City surroundings. Wren's knowledge of geometry enabled him to create sensations of depth, space and light that one might have thought impossible, and St Stephen's is an outstanding example of his skill in dealing with such a restricted ground area. The church's nearest neighbour is the mid-eighteenth-century Palladian-style Mansion House that is the official residence of London's Lord Mayor. The two buildings stand so close together that from certain angles it is impossible to actually notice that there is a green dome set on the roof of St Stephen Walbrook's.

Entry into the main body of the church is via a flight of steps and heavily framed door, through which one is then presented with Wren's masterpiece. The interior is a perfect rectangle divided into bays, aisles and a sanctuary by the introduction of sixteen equal-sized Corinthian columns. By walking into the main body of the church past an initial line of four columns, the remainder can then be observed forming a centralizing plan in four groups of three in the corners.

However, the fascinating thing about Wren's construction is that although the columns support a circular dome, they also form a Greek Cross out of the transepts, nave and chancel. The inner square then becomes an octagon by the device of throwing arches across the corners and it is on those eight columns that the dome and its lantern rest.

St Stephen Walbrook's structure was patently intended as a dress rehearsal for the dome of St Paul's Cathedral. Although Wren was thought to be working on both designs during that period, the domes were actually quite different in the manner and style of their construction. St Stephen's was based on a lighter combination of wood and plaster but, even so, its columns still had to support a weight of over eight tonnes.

With every step taken around the original church, the perspective changed, and now even more so since its interior was redesigned in the latter decades of the twentieth century. However, the first stage in its transformation was actually the late eighteenth-century removal of the high box pews due to dry rot as they were the items of standard church furniture upon which Wren had based his column dimensions. The church was then quite badly damaged during the Second World War, but its survival hung seriously in the balance

Many London churches have the power to create an initial, breathtaking moment of visual impact, but one guaranteed to actually cause congestion at the entrance door is this Wren masterpiece. The dome is spectacular but almost equally matched by the complex geometric layout of soaring Corinthian columns.

decades later when significant damage and underground erosion caused by the River Walbrook was discovered by the churchwarden Lord Peter Palumbo. It was his drive and generosity that enabled St Stephen's to be rescued and preserved for the future during a major restoration project from 1978–87. He also caused anxiety in some quarters because he had not simply funded the structural restoration but also proclaimed that the layout of the church was to be changed.

In 1972, he had commissioned the world-famous sculptor Henry Moore to create a new altar that would be set in the centre of the church directly beneath the dome. This altar was not a complex creation, but rather an eight-tonne piece of travertine marble. There was a great deal of angst at this radical change and it took two Ecclesiastical Court hearings to get official approval for its addition. The vicar of St Stephen Walbrook, Chad Varah (1911–2007), had been in his post since 1953 and was a great supporter of the new scheme as he deemed it a far more sociable way to conduct communion services. The world actually owes an awful lot to the Reverend Chad Varah, as it was he who founded the Samaritans shortly after joining St Stephen Walbrook, and the original black telephone used for saving many lives still sits in a glass case at the back of the church.

St Stephen's interior is crowned by a dome that was the forerunner of Wren's work on St Paul's Cathedral. Most architects had to rely on drawings and scale models before undertaking the actual construction, but the rebuilding of London after the Great Fire gave him life-sized opportunities.

56 Great Churches of London

ST STEPHEN WALBROOK 57

OPPOSITE An intricate, tiled mosaic of St Stephen adorns the entrance stairs leading up to the church. He is venerated as being the first Christian martyr and was stoned to death around 33–36 CE, having been accused of 'blasphemy' by the Jewish authorities who did not like or agree with his Christian teachings.

ABOVE Set directly beneath the dome is St Stephen's beautiful but controversial altar, sculpted from travertine marble by Henry Moore in 1972. The altar is encircled by the dazzling coloured kneelers designed in 1993 by Patrick Heron and created by Tapisserie, the specialists in hand-painted needlework.

St Martin-within-Ludgate

LUDGATE HILL, EC4

Although set on the banks of the Thames, London nevertheless has quite a few significant undulations not far from the river and one of the most visually atmospheric is Ludgate Hill. From the junction of Fleet Street and Farringdon Street it gradually climbs up to the majestic outline of St Paul's Cathedral. From that initial viewpoint there is a beautiful visual contrast between the mighty bulk of St Paul's and the needle-thin dark spire of St Martin's. If one makes that gradual ascent on foot, it is actually possible to walk straight past the church, as its street-level stone frontage is of the same tonal value as its neighbours and there are no graphic pieces of carved stonework on either side of the main doorway.

Ludgate was one of the original seven gates piercing London's Roman Wall and this one was demolished in 1760. St Martin-within-Ludgate was first mentioned in 1174, rebuilt in the mid-fifteenth century and then consumed by the Great Fire of 1666. It was one of the last City churches on Sir Christopher Wren's post-Fire schedule, with work beginning in 1677 and completed seven years later. Wren moved the construction site slightly north to enable part of the redundant Wall to be incorporated into the church's west end. The south façade's main entrance starts with three bays built with pale Portland stone, the central one comprising a slightly projecting tower, linked to the ones on either side by large angled scrolls. That all serves as a symmetrical frame incorporating three large windows set below, and creates a perfect launch pad for the complexity of the final stages leading up to the dark, beautifully slender spire.

St Martin-within-Ludgate is a perfect example of Wren's ability to combine the practical elements of building with architectural and artistic design, and creating such a spire served as a perfect visual foil to the mighty dome of nearby St Paul's Cathedral. The internal space was also slightly difficult to manage and Wren opted for a Greek Cross format set within a square, the cross being defined by four Corinthian columns, whose lower wood sections are now excessively tall and dark due to the removal of earlier box pews. That wood was 'recycled' to create the current pews and choir stalls, all adorned with intricate carving. The perfectly square geometry of the interior was enabled by the creation of a large entrance lobby from the street, with three very heavy and artistically carved doors. That double 'audio barricade' of a stone exterior wall and those substantial doors ensured an interior well protected from traffic noise, be it hooves and carriage wheels or buses and taxis.

So much of the interior has remained more or less as it was due to St Martin-within-Ludgate's escape from Second World War damage. It was struck by just one incendiary bomb that did no harm, and was therefore one of the least damaged City churches. That meant that most items of furnishing that were part of the original church are still an integral part of it. One of the most captivating features is the amount of scrolled woodwork, and the altar, font and pulpit are adorned with impeccably crafted balusters. Another intricately decorated

---

The magnificent trio of St Paul's dome and tower combined with St Martin's contrasting dark, slender spire creates one of the City's best architectural compositions. Unfortunately, that visual perfection has sadly been tarnished by the over-prominent curved façade of an office building in the foreground.

item that essentially looks like a cabinet with open bookshelves was originally called a 'bread shelf' as it was created to enable the more wealthy parishioners to leave loaves of bread for the poor. The east end with the altar and reredos looks particularly atmospheric due to its floor levels being raised during a major late nineteenth-century restoration in which black and white tiles were used in ascending levels to create a great colour contrast with all the dark wood. The rails surrounding the altar are actually set quite high and were apparently done so to 'keep people and dogs away from the altar and give it respect'.

St Martin-within-Ludgate is no longer a parish church and became a Guild Church in 1954. Eight years later it was also chosen to become the Chapel of the Honourable Society of the Knights of the Round Table. It was founded by actors, artists and writers as a means of maintaining the values established by the legendary King Arthur, and one of its most significant early members was Charles Dickens.

Sir Christopher Wren was obviously widely acclaimed for the creation of St Paul's Cathedral, but its diminutive next-door neighbour, St Martin-within-Ludgate, still ranks highly in his church portfolio. The only visual blemishes are the stained glass windows now blocking out essential light as Wren was definitely a clear glass designer.

BELOW The west end gallery housing the church organ provides a great view down into Wren's Greek Cross interior.

OPPOSITE The elegantly carved and gold-inscribed reredos creates a perfect aesthetic backdrop to the altar and redesigned stepped flooring added during a nineteenth-century restoration.

St Martin-within-Ludgate 61

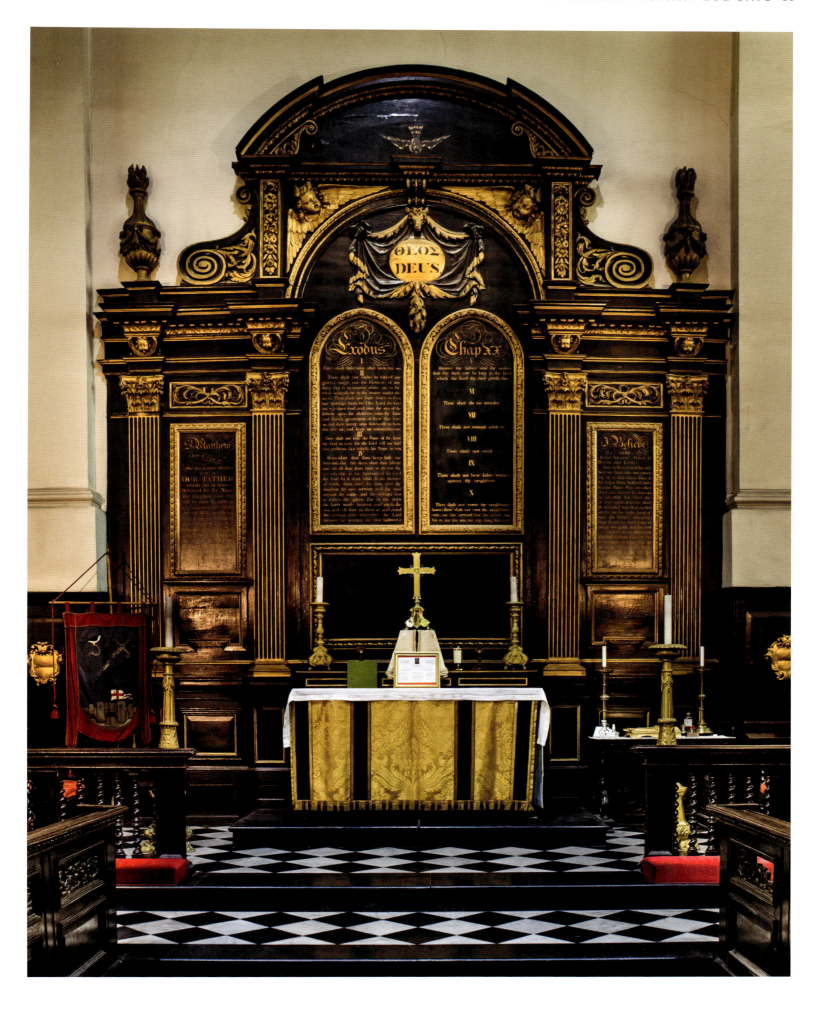

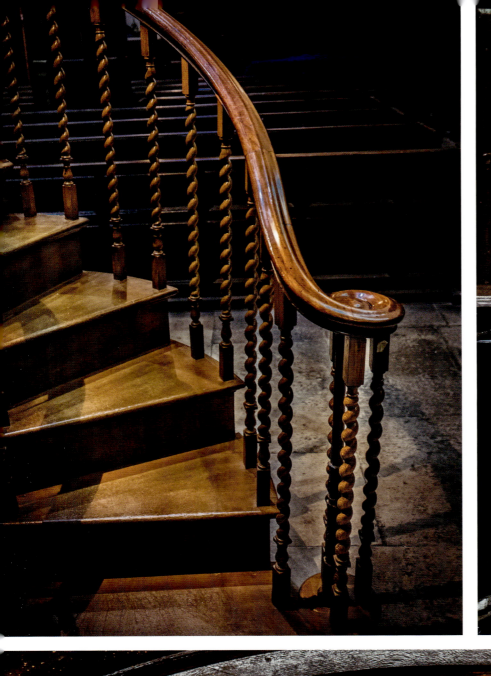
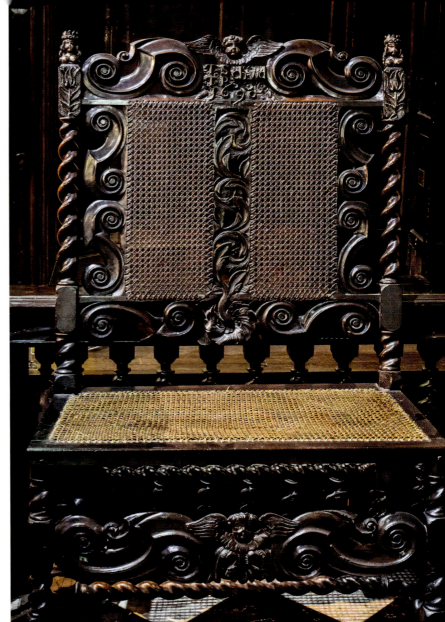
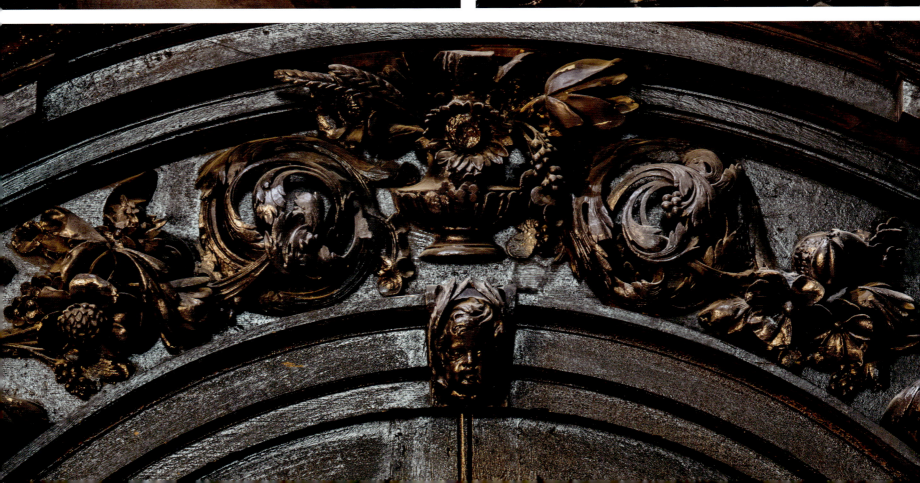

ST MARTIN-WITHIN-LUDGATE 63

OPPOSITE: ABOVE LEFT The pulpit's curved steps are supported by finely turned wooden balusters. ABOVE RIGHT The late seventeenth-century double churchwarden's chair is a very rare piece of church furniture. BOTTOM The sublimely carved pediment over one of the three vestibule doors.

ABOVE A seventeenth-century carved figure of a female pelican depicted feeding its young with blood from her pierced breast to avoid their starvation during harsh times. This was a very early Christian representation of Jesus's Sacrifice found in quite a few of the older London churches.

St Mary Abchurch

ABCHURCH LANE, EC4

St Mary Abchurch is located on a narrow lane linking Cannon Street with King William Street. Its origins date back to the twelfth century when it belonged to the Augustinian Priory of St Mary Overie set on the south bank of the River Thames, the site now occupied by Southwark Cathedral. Following the Reformation, the patronage was transferred to Corpus Christi College in Cambridge, and St Mary Abchurch ultimately became a Guild Church in 1952. There seems to be no definitive explanation regarding the 'Abchurch' part of St Mary's name, although it has been suggested that the medieval priory canons might just have simply referred to St Mary's as the 'Up church' as it was set on rising ground above the river.

The area directly in front of the church called St Mary's Yard was originally a burial site and now serves as an outdoor venue for a neighbouring pub and restaurant. To the left side of the church, that open space diminishes into a narrow enclosed passageway, having an atmospheric feel that transports one back to the time when much of London was built in such a tight fashion. It also generates an impression of how easy it must have been for the flames of the Great Fire of London in 1666 to so rapidly consume the City, especially at a time when wood was such a significant building material.

Sir Christopher Wren was commissioned to rebuild the church, with construction beginning in 1681 and completed some five years later. The red brick exterior has a simple tower with a lead spire and an elegant grouping of windows on the south front. Although that ensemble is not overly dramatic, it follows the Wren tradition of geometric and design simplicity when in a space restricted location. The church interior is virtually square and remains one of the City's least altered churches, having luckily lost only its box pews during the Victorian era. St Mary Abchurch has a stunning portfolio of woodcarving, with the most impressive piece being a reredos set behind the altar that was the work of Grinling Gibbons (1648–1721). The artistry is quite extraordinary, and a lot of his delicate carvings of fruits and flowers are accomplished in a style that just would not be feasible in stone. Scattered around the City of London and even further afield, churches were claiming that a particularly fine piece of woodcarving was a 'Gibbons masterpiece' but, unlike St Mary Abchurch, they would not be able to supply a receipt as confirmatory evidence. One of the more curious, much published stories concerning the reredos was the 'fact' that it was smashed into smithereens by a wartime bomb blast. The thousands of fragments were then all gathered up and later pieced together as though nothing had happened. What actually did happen was that when war broke out, the reredos and other treasures were removed from the church and stored well away from the City.

Another significant part of the great wood carving collection is the pulpit dominated by a massive sounding board, designed and executed by William Grey, although one wonders how that extremely large tester could be supported by just one rear pillar.

The magnificent Grinling Gibbons reredos (altar piece) fills the east end of the church. Gibbons used pale lime wood for most of his work, and it is so sad that the Victorians stained and varnished it, thereby making his incredible detail less visible.

ST MARY ABCHURCH

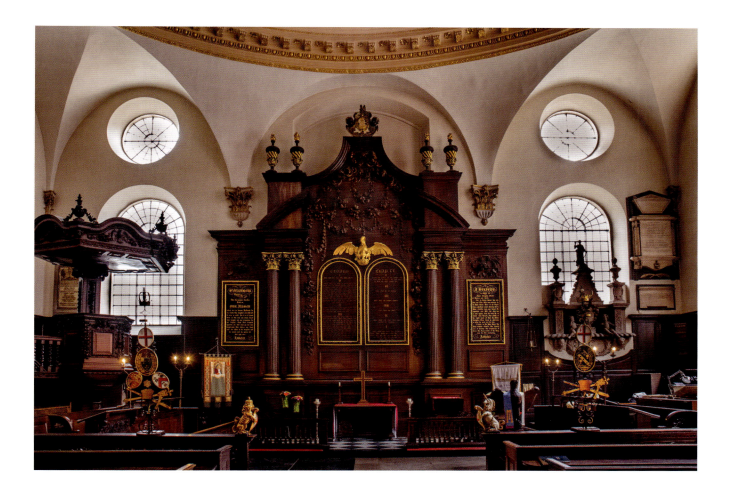

Up on the roof of the church there is none of the usual visual evidence accompanying a dome's construction but, as this was all happening in the 1680s, St Mary Abchurch was another element of Wren's practical research ahead of the rebuilding of St Paul's Cathedral. Essentially, the dome is not supported by the customary set of pillars but, in a clever piece of architectural engineering, simply rests upon eight modest arches springing from the church walls. The dome's painting was done by parishioner William Snow in 1708 and features the name of God in Hebrew lettering, worshipping angels and portrayals of the Christian Virtues. Although damaged by a bomb blast during the Blitz, it was successfully restored and retouched. The walls of the church are copiously lined with a fascinating portfolio of memorials from the post-Great Fire centuries, and the detailed craftsmanship of all the monuments and furnishings are well illuminated by the massive, plain glass south window.

St Mary Abchurch is the home of The Friends of London Churches, an architectural charity dedicated to preserving the City churches and ensuring that as many as possible are regularly open to both visitors and worshippers. If the charity did not exist, the chances of being able to savour the architecture and art treasures of City churches would be significantly reduced.

OPPOSITE: TOP LEFT Unicorns were displayed as Christian symbols of purity and sacrifice. TOP RIGHT A detail of superb carving on the pulpit. BOTTOM LEFT The Virgin and Child embroidered on a processional banner placed by the altar. BOTTOM RIGHT A ceremonial sword rest.

ABOVE The view down London City's least altered church is a truly mesmerizing experience comprising Sir Christopher Wren's symmetrical perfection, Grinling Gibbons' reredos, the pulpit's portfolio of carving, and the seventeenth-century memorial to Sir Patience Ward, Lord Mayor of London in 1681.

68 GREAT CHURCHES OF LONDON

ABOVE Although much of the church's finest carved pieces are centred around the altar, there are two magnificent chandeliers rising up from each set of pews. Although now lit safely by electricity rather than candles, the lighting is nevertheless gloriously atmospheric.

OPPOSITE William Snow's 1708 painting within the dome created by Sir Christopher Wren shows, in the centre, the Tetragrammaton (the name of God in Hebrew), surrounded by the rays of Glory, a colourful chorus of worshipping angels and, in monochrome, the figures of the Christian Virtues.

St Clement Danes

STRAND, WC2

There are always various explanations as to how churches acquired their full titles, and the St Clement part is straightforward. He was a first-century Pope of Rome who upset Emperor Trajan through the Christian conversion of many slaves and was executed by having his neck attached to a ship's anchor and thrown overboard. The 'Danes' element seems to hover around several historical options relating to pre-Conquest Danish settlers. The most likely outcome was that they were granted permission to occupy this particular part of London, subsequently married native English women, then settled down and built a church. It was rebuilt by William the Conqueror and repaired through the later Medieval era, and St Clement's came to no harm in the Great Fire of 1666.

However, although the church had escaped fire damage, it was in a most parlous state anyway and, despite his extensive workload, Sir Christopher Wren designed and organized its rebuilding in 1680. He was predominantly involved in the main body of the church and, with the exception of St Paul's Cathedral, St Clement Danes was actually his only rebuilt church with an east end apse. He entrusted the tower building to one of his close colleagues Joshua Marshall, and the steeple was created in 1719 by James Gibbs, who was also responsible for St Mary le Strand (page 102) and St Martin-in-the-Fields (page 108). Another key member of Sir Christopher Wren's associates was the architectural sculptor Edward Pearce, who transformed the interior design from drawings into the reality of stone, wood and glass.

Unfortunately, those efforts were eventually wiped out by incendiary bombs during a Second World War bombing raid (there is a dramatic black and white photo of that moment displayed in the church). Because the damage was by fire, rather than explosion, the church walls and tower survived in a vaguely 'restorable' state, but nothing in terms of rebuilding actually happened for another decade. Progress was eventually made and St Clement Danes was transformed from a skeletal, weed-clad stone shell into a glorious reproduction of Wren's original that was designated as the Central Church of the RAF. It was reconsecrated in 1958 in a service attended by Queen Elizabeth II and the Duke of Edinburgh.

As one enters through the west door, the colour contrast and symmetry of the layout is absolutely perfect. The use of dark woodwork is visually dramatic and well lit by gallery windows not overloaded or darkened by stained glass. As they run down the nave, the first-floor galleries are narrowed down to physically and visually encompass the semi-circular apse. It comprises the altar and a curved reredos that has two arched panels representing the Annunciation painted by Ruskin Spear. The apse's domed ceiling is geometrically patterned and works well with the large sculpted Stuart Royal Arms on the east arch. All this beautiful composition is enhanced by the hundreds of RAF squadron badges carved from Welsh slate and laid to create the nave floor. Just inside the west door the large heraldic emblem of the RAF is set into the floor and surrounded by the badges of the Commonwealth Air Forces

The steeple of St Clement Danes was designed in 1719 by James Gibbs (1682–1754) and was an early work from an architect who was destined for a hugely successful career in many different fields of architecture. The steeple is elegant, intricate – and very high.

who helped in the war. The north aisle is enriched with the visually striking emblem of the Polish Air Force who fought alongside their British counterparts.

The walls around the aisles are lined with glass cases containing memorial books to the many, many thousands who died in the protection of their nation during the Second World War and other conflicts. There is also a large memorial book of remembrance dedicated to the large number of American airmen based in this country who also sacrificed their lives for our protection.

St Clement Danes is set on a traffic-free 'island' and there are some exterior memorial statues respecting significant figures in both peace and war. At the east end stands a memorial to Samuel Johnson (1709–84), creator of the first major English dictionary. At the west end are two figures related to the RAF's war history: Air Chief Marshal Lord Dowding was head of Fighter Command during the Battle of Britain and Sir Arthur 'Bomber' Harris was in charge of Bomber Command.

On a more peaceful level, there actually is still conflict and dispute between St Clement Danes and St Clement's Eastcheap, both insisting that it was their church being sung about in the nursery rhyme 'Oranges and lemons, say the bells of St Clement's'. All one could say is that Eastcheap is considerably closer to the Thames quays where citrus fruit was once unloaded, but who knows?

OPPOSITE The east window was the work of Carl Edwards (1914–85), born in London to Finnish parents and who had always been in the world of glass. He was a member of the Worshipful Company of Glaziers (founded in 1328) and won their annual prize in 1947–8.

BELOW Pew ends display the cartouches of many Chiefs of the Air Staff, and hooked onto the back of each pew are kneelers whose covers have been created by family or friends in memory of airmen who died in defence of the nation. OVERLEAF The interior of St Clement Danes.

ST CLEMENT DANES 77

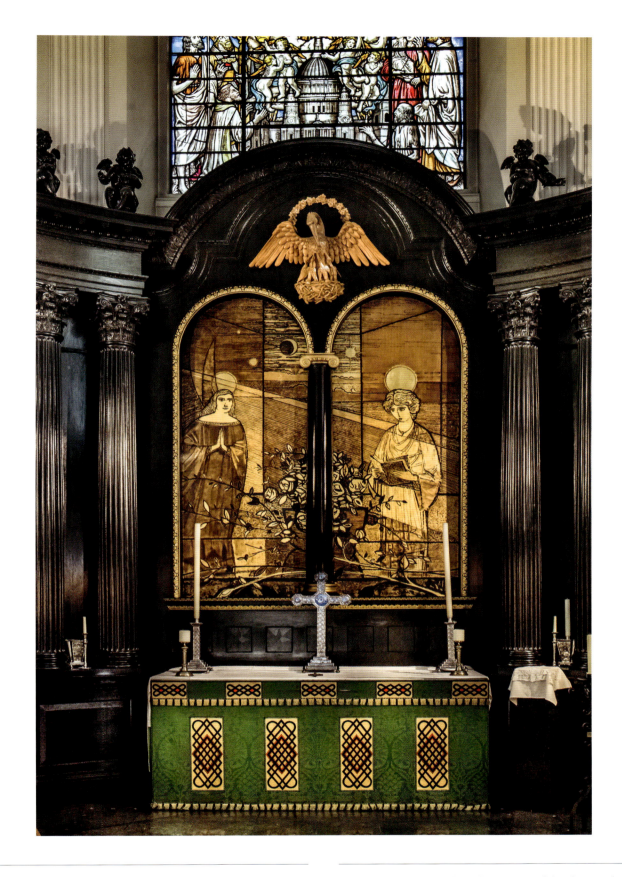

OPPOSITE The final line of pews at the church's west end are elaborately decorated and reserved for senior officials and Air Force commanders during formal and ceremonial services. Directly above is the impressive organ, a gift from the United States Air Force and installed in 1958.

ABOVE The reredos is adorned with a graceful and atmospheric portrayal of the Annunciation with a pelican of piety set above by the British artist Ruskin Spear CBE (1911–90). He was one of thirty-eight official artists commissioned by the War Artists Advisory Commission and produced several works between 1942–4.

St Mary Aldermary

BOW LANE, EC4

St Mary Aldermary is located less than 800 metres (½ mile to the east of St Paul's Cathedral on Watling Street, one of the more familiar names of England's Roman road network. It extended from the English Channel port of Dover, up through London past St Mary's and then north-west to Wroxeter near the Welsh border. The other street adjoining the church is Bow Lane, named after St Mary-le-Bow, a church also dedicated to the Virgin Mary lying just a short distance away. Although it does not always work, linguistic logic veers towards the fact that 'Aldermary' means that this church is simply 'older' than the other. Whatever type of church had existed on this site during the post-Conquest and early Medieval periods, surviving records show that it was definitely rebuilt around 1510 under the patronage of Lord Mayor Henry Keble, who then passed away just eight years later. Repeated lack of funding caused periodic delays, but work restarted on building the substantial tower in 1530. However, further fluctuations in financial support from benefactors meant that it was not until 1629 that the final stone was laid. Just thirty-seven years later, the Great Fire of London swept through the City; the tower largely survived the blaze but suffered further damage during the hurricane-status storm of 1703 that caused utter mayhem and destruction throughout the south of England.

If the tower had not been so robustly built and survived the Fire, one wonders whether it would have retained that particular square format with ladder-style corners when Sir Christopher Wren started to rebuild the church in 1679. Interestingly, a plaque on the church wall explains that St Mary Aldermary is a Guild Church, and also states that it was 'Rebuilt by Wren's Office', rather than just using his name. It is quite possible that the wording was simply a formal way of writing, because when one does get to fully appreciate the church's interior, there would probably have been only just the one person in that office who could have created such a breathtaking portfolio of design and decoration.

The most surprising aspect of that interior is that it was created largely in the Gothic Perpendicular style, which made St Mary's the sole post-Fire parish church to have been built in that manner. Most of the rebuilt churches were created through a chosen architect drawing up the plan, submitting it to the Fifty New Churches Commissioners and parish officials, and then only proceeding if sanctioned. St Mary Aldermary had both a caring parish and individual financial contributors, all of whom requested that the church be rebuilt in the same Gothic style in which it had been created. The established late Perpendicular rectangular plan was followed, apart from the slightly angled east wall that was off centre because it had been a surviving segment of the fire-damaged church. There were six bay arcades and wide aisles but no chancel. However, from the moment one steps into the church interior, the eyes are hypnotically drawn upwards to the sheer majesty and complexity of the fan vaulting.

There are no surviving parish or church records that might have given an indication as to whether Wren was amending

---

The church tower is still not dominated by the monumental office buildings that have risen in so many other parts of the City. Its top elements, called finials, were originally in stone but in 1962 were replaced by lighter, and thereby safer, gold-coated fibreglass replicas.

the design of a lavish pre-Fire vault or starting from scratch but, either way, the outcome is a remarkable work of art. On balance it would seem that some aspects of the design are very 'Wren-like' and would not have been included in a regulation Perpendicular design. The vaults are all plaster and cover the nave and both aisles. The fans do not extend across the vaults in the previously accepted Gothic manner, but embrace large, traceried saucers enriched with cusping (see overleaf).

The Victorians became renowned for their London church 'restorations', and in 1876 much of the beautiful seventeenth-century woodwork was removed in a rather heavy-handed method of apparently winding the design clock back to the Medieval period. Fortunately, the pulpit, an imposing official wooden sword rest and the font and its cover were all deemed sufficiently tasteful and ancient to be left in place. The church did suffer bomb damage during the Blitz, which blew out all the windows and did some damage to the fan vaulting, most of which has since been renovated. Since 2012, a rear section of the nave has been transformed into an ethical, non-profit-making coffee shop run by St Mary Aldermary. There could not be a more atmospheric place in which to relax and savour such a captivating portfolio of church architecture.

OPPOSITE: TOP LEFT Virgin and Child by Lawrence Lee (1909–2011) in the south chapel's east window. BOTTOM LEFT An intricately carved pew end that survived the Victorian 'restorations'. RIGHT The original organ was built in 1781 by England and Russell, then rebuilt and enlarged in 1877.

ABOVE The main altar backed by a reredos that was installed during the Victorian period restoration. OVERLEAF A view down the nave's central aisle towards the west window, with the visually stunning fan vaulting benefiting from extra light generated by the clerestory glass.

Christ Church, Spitalfields

COMMERCIAL STREET, E1

Christ Church, Spitalfields is universally acknowledged as the finest of Nicholas Hawksmoor's six London churches. The best vantage point from which to fully appreciate the beauty of this architectural masterpiece is Brushfield Street, the main thoroughfare running alongside the historical market of Spitalfields, a name derived from the nearby twelfth-century priory and hospital of St Mary Spital. This area of London lies just outside the City's north-eastern boundary, and in the late seventeenth-century, post-Fire era it started to become quite heavily populated. The most significant influx came from France, when vast numbers of the Protestant Huguenots fled across the Channel to escape religious persecution. They were renowned silk weavers, and that industry grew and flourished around Spitalfields. The Huguenots then started building their own chapels of worship.

The rapid population expansion in this district and elsewhere around London resulted in the establishing in 1711 of the Commission for Building Fifty New Churches, and it was decided to grant three new churches in this area to cater for such a significant rise in numbers. It was also seen as a necessary measure to ensure that this expanding community had religious unity, and Nicholas Hawksmoor was commissioned to design all three (Christ Church Spitalfields, St Anne's Limehouse and St George's in the East at Upper Wapping). The Spitalfields site was bought in 1713 and construction began the following year upon the approval of Hawksmoor's submitted design. However, work ground to a halt a few years later as debts mounted, and it was not until well into the 1720s that significant progress was made, the spire constructed, and Christ Church was finally consecrated by the Bishop of London on 7 July 1729.

Unlike many nearby City churches, Christ Church is not hemmed in by office blocks, so every architectural and artistic element is clearly visible from all angles. The north, east and south façades all have their individual characteristics based largely upon the varying window formats. Each was designed to maximize available light sources, and ensure a perfect combination of both practical and aesthetic lighting inside the church, and visually appealing geometry on the exterior. However, as with most other churches, the west end is the architectural showcase, and at Christ Church Hawksmoor did not hold back with his design and execution, much to the chagrin of those who deemed that not adhering to the absolute fixed elements of Classical design was architectural blasphemy.

A flight of steps leads up to the west entrance, comprising a vast portico of four massive Tuscan columns with a central circular arch. The width of the portico is continued upwards by the tower's square buttresses, which then give way to an imposing temple that actually looks a bit more Gothic than Classical. Sadly, it was actually simplified in an early nineteenth-century restoration after fire caused significant, but not irreparable damage. The elegant spire rises to a height of 68.5m (225ft), and when that entire west front is lit by crisp sunlight, polarized sunglasses are highly recommended.

Christ Church Spitalfields literally towers above the historic Spitalfields Market, and whether viewed from a distance or up close, the architectural style and composition of Nicholas Hawksmoor's eighteenth-century masterpiece is utterly captivating.

86　Great Churches of London

The Industrial Revolution started in 1760, and that date signalled the gradual decline of Spitalfields as its hand silk weaving industry was essentially made redundant as machinery replaced human skills. Many other industries were similarly affected, and the level of poverty rose so rapidly throughout the nineteenth century that hardly any money could be spared for essential church repairs and maintenance. That decline escalated, and by the mid-twentieth century the roof and other parts had deteriorated to such a dangerous extent that the church was closed for public worship in 1958.

The dreaded word 'demolition' began to be muttered but, fortunately, a pair of the right kind of ears heard it and as a result those proposals were quashed. That enabled the newly founded Hawksmoor Committee to avert demolition and the Church of England funded the vital first-aid treatment of reroofing. Thereafter, an organization named the Friends of Christ Church Spitalfields was formed and became the registered charity that literally brought Nicholas Hawksmoor's architectural gem back to life. It took a long time and a huge amount of money but, as a result of two significant donations from the National Lottery Fund, help from English Heritage and other charities, the church was not only saved but literally reborn. Terrible procedures had been inflicted during the Victoria era, including the removal of galleries, and more also happened in the twentieth century. The Friends studied Hawksmoor's original plans, and the absolutely mesmerizing interior that exists today is the church he actually designed and built.

Daylight floods into the church interior through many windows, and any harshness is softly tempered by atmospheric chandeliers. The sheer beauty of Hawksmoor's impressive composition of pillars, arches and the large beam over the chancel supporting a royal coat of arms is accentuated by the absence of pews.

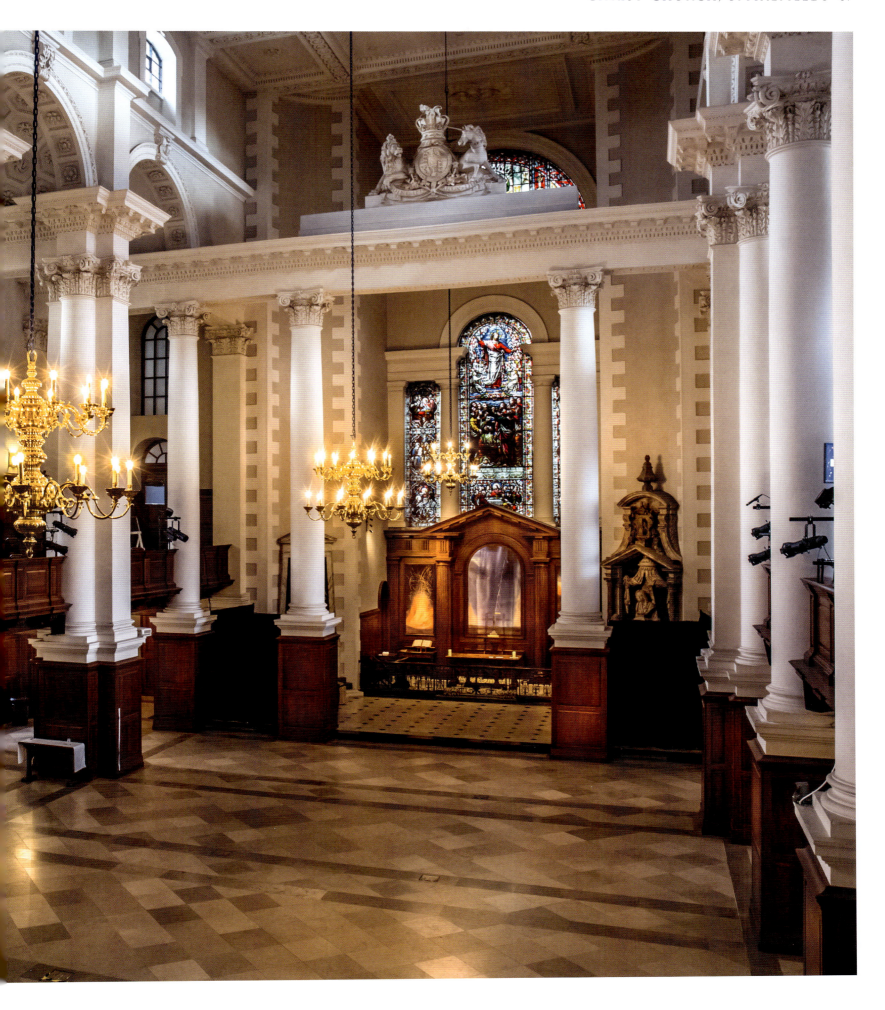

88 Great Churches of London

above left The Venetian east end window rising up behind the altar was created by the Soho studio of Ward & Hughes in 1876. The Nativity is one of six side panels, with the main centre piece portraying the Resurrection.
above right One of the intricately carved nave column capitals.

opposite The east end is such an exquisite example of Hawksmoor's creative interior design. The chancel is defined by the addition of two extra nave columns that perfectly frame the altar, with the lighting being a subtle combination from the stained glass and an overhead chandelier.

St Mary Woolnoth

LOMBARD STREET, EC3

Unlike some of its neighbouring churches lying partially hidden in the heart of the City, St Mary Woolnoth stands proud and undaunted by the soaring invasions of concrete, stone and glass. There has been a church here since the twelfth century, although the earliest records are somewhat vague, and varied options exist regarding the origins of its name. It could have been from an early benefactor named Wulfnoth, or maybe derived from its close proximity to a wool-weighing yard as 'noth' was a corruption of the word 'neath' meaning 'near'. The earliest confirmation that there was a church bearing its current name was in the latter decades of the thirteenth century. It was rebuilt two centuries later and then badly damaged in the Great Fire of 1666. Although repaired by Sir Christopher Wren, it soon fell into decay and the parishioners campaigned for a rebuilding under the 'Fifty New Churches Act' of 1710 that was to be funded by a coal tax. The church of St Mary Woolnoth was built between 1716 and 1727 by Nicholas Hawksmoor, who began his architectural career at the age of eighteen as an assistant to Sir Christopher Wren. He moved rapidly from the status of protégé to exceptional colleague, and his influence can be seen in the verve and vitality of Wren's later work. Hawksmoor realized his own distinctive fusion of Classical authority and Gothic fancy in his six great London churches, St Mary Woolnoth actually being the only one within the City.

The dramatic west front is set on the junction of King William and Lombard streets and, at first glance, could not be immediately classified as a church. The substantial lower storey comprises an arched entrance portal, above which is a set of Corinthian columns, and the final stage has two small towers linked by a short balustrade. St Mary Woolnoth actually had to be erected differently on each side due to the eighteenth-century street layout. The north façade on Lombard Street houses three large niches enclosing Corinthian columns supported on concave pedestals. The south side is different again, having been more simply designed due to its location next to a narrow alley because King William Street did not appear until a century later.

The red and blue sign indicating an Underground station gleams out against the dark stone, and it was towards the end of the nineteenth century that the City & South London Railway sought to acquire the church. There were delays and disagreements but, in the end, the outcome was favourable to both parties. Hawksmoor's church was saved and the rail company got the crypt, which is now the Northern line's Bank station ticket hall. The church was structurally strengthened with underground metalwork, and the priests and congregation became significantly healthier than they were prior to the crypt being emptied of very many corpses. On some days the interior was pleasant enough, but there were times when the vicar found it difficult to deliver prayers and sermons with his sore throat. The bodies removed were reinterred into a mass grave at the City of London Cemetery in Ilford, and St Mary Woolnoth was actually one of the most highly populated of the crypt-bearing City churches.

St Mary Woolnoth occupies such a prominent position in the heart of the City that it has had to endure several attempted demolitions during the nineteenth and twentieth centuries. Its role as parish church for the Lord Mayors of London has helped its survival.

92 GREAT CHURCHES OF LONDON

Given the size and dramatic appearance of its main frontage, the church interior is actually quite small and one simply walks into what started out as a square box. However, being a 'Hawksmoor' church, that simple format was creatively structured and became a box within a box through the addition of four sets of triple Corinthian columns. That definition of the internal space thereby created a clerestory, each side of which had a semi-circular window, the light from which is boosted by a large central chandelier. The altar is set in front of a dramatic black and gold reredos flanked by elegant twisted columns, reminiscent of the one created by Bernini for St Peter's in Rome.

The church is lined with many memorial plaques, the most notable being the one dedicated to the Reverend John Newton (1725–1807), vicar of the church from 1780 until his death. During his early years he had been involved in the African slave trade, but later became an abolitionist, and one of his parishioners was William Wilberforce (1759–1833), who was so inspired by Newton's sermons and collaboration that he worked even harder to get slavery abolished. The Rev. John Newton was also a prolific hymn writer, and undoubtedly his most popular composition that still echoes around the world today (albeit with a different tune) was 'Amazing Grace'.

ABOVE The design layout of Nicholas Hawksmoor's interior is just so sublimely symmetrical, with every single element sitting perfectly matching its neighbour or the wall and window opposite.

OPPOSITE Even though the three Corinthian columns are really substantial, they do not visually overwhelm the other furnishings. The architect William Butterfield (1814–1900) worked on the church in the 1870s on projects that included cutting down the box pews.

OPPOSITE In addition to his own geometric layout, Hawksmoor was equally attached to ensuring artistic detail by craftsmen, and the wood pulpit carvings equally matched the intricacies of the acanthus leaves and scrolls decorating the Corinthian columns. Architect William Butterfield patently made a mistake during his restoration work by lowering the pulpit but not following that down with the tester, thereby diminishing its effectiveness as a sounding board.

ABOVE Walking around the ambulatory is a fascinating experience as the perspective changes with every step. Standing immediately in front of a column almost blocks out the rest of the church, but then seeing a cluster at the other end seems more of an artistic element. Visiting at dusk or on a dull day allows the chandelier and subsidiary lighting to cast a wonderfully atmospheric glow.

St George's

BLOOMSBURY WAY, WC1

St George's sits on the north side of Bloomsbury Way and very close to the British Museum. It was the last church built for the 'Fifty New Churches Act' of 1710, created to provide places of worship for a burgeoning population whose religious needs were being vastly under-served in many districts. However, what looked good on paper did not quite match the reality, and just twelve new churches were built, with a few extras created from repair and modification. This was arguably Nicholas Hawksmoor's greatest venture into the world of Classical architecture and, although never actually having travelled to Europe, he fervently studied drawings and engravings of the past. In 1714 the Commissioners overseeing the New Churches programme were being implored to create a church in the increasingly fashionable Bloomsbury district. It was set on the northern fringes of the St Giles-in-the-Fields parish, and to access their church meant a risky journey for parishioners down through the 'Rookery' (roughly around what is now the New Oxford Street area), which was then one of the worst and most dangerous slum districts of London.

Several leading architects were asked to submit plans, but Hawksmoor's design was accepted and work commenced in 1716. The main problem to be addressed was the physical restrictiveness of the site that is now even more tightly pressed by large buildings on either side. The location did not really fulfil the criteria established by the Commission, which required churches to be visibly prominent and to architecturally dominate their surroundings. Hemmed in it may be, but St George's main south-facing façade is a visually imposing deep portico of columns raised above a flight of steps. One would normally expect a church tower to then soar symmetrically above that entrance, but Hawksmoor set his tower on the west side so that it did not visually compete with the south façade.

The portico may have comprised pure Corinthian columns with correctly sculpted capitals, but Hawksmoor's steeple swerved slightly off course. It was set upon the short square tower built with four sides of columns that mirrored the south front, but the actual steeple was created from a different style of ancient monument. He modelled the stepped pyramid on descriptions of one of the Seven Wonders of the Ancient World, the Mausoleum at Halicarnassus in Turkey. However, that ancient monument certainly did not include lions and unicorns clambering around the base of its steeple, and it transpired that Hawksmoor had seemingly 'forgotten' to tell the Commission that they were to be included. The steeple is finally topped by a statue of King George I (r. 1714–27) and the church was consecrated on 28 January 1730 by Edmund Gibson, Bishop of London.

Architecturally, Hawksmoor was pressured to ensure that the layout of the church was in the traditional east-west orientation and that did cause significant problems due to lack of space. Categorically stating that he would achieve that condition won him the contract, so the design burden was quite heavy. He therefore had to create an entrance through

---

St George's in Bloomsbury has got to be seriously considered as the finest of Hawksmoor's six London churches created under the Fifty Churches Act, and probably unique as no other church architect has ever drawn images of unicorns and lions on his plans.

the west tower so that parishioners entering the church faced the altar set in the east end's semi-circular apse. However, the church officials soon became unhappy with the fact that its restrictive east-west arrangement was not providing sufficient accommodation, and it was therefore eventually reset on a north-south axis. That created an additional 337 seats to boost the original capacity of 447 up to a more acceptable level.

Hawksmoor originally fitted the interior with north- and south-facing galleries that would separately accommodate the two most important parishioners, the Dukes of Bedford and Montagu and their respective family members. East and west galleries had also been erected at some point but were dismantled and removed by the Victorian architect G.E. Street, who also decided that lions and unicorns had no place on a church spire and so they were removed in 1871.

Although having served as the University of London's church from 1956–68, St George's thereafter struggled to maintain its role as a significant parish church and gradually started to physically decay. There were several localized attempts to renovate parts of the church, but thankfully its increasingly parlous state was brought to the attention of the World Monuments Fund and also added to the English Heritage Buildings at Risk register. Nine million pounds was secured for its restoration and the interior layout was returned to Hawksmoor's original east-west format. The Victorian pews were replaced with bespoke oak benches and the steeple was once again clad with newly sculpted lions and unicorns.

The early twenty-first-century restoration saved the church's fabric and also returned it to the original layout devised by Nicholas Hawksmoor. The seventeenth-century Dutch chandelier loaned from the Victoria and Albert Museum is such a beautiful and atmospherically perfect addition.

100 Great Churches of London

above Most of the stained glass in the church today dates back to the Victorian restoration work during the late nineteenth century. This particular portrait of one of the Apostles was created by the renowned London glass-making firm of Clayton & Bell.

opposite The only grand monument in the church is set by the west tower entrance and commemorates Charles Grant (1746–1823), who was chairman of the East India Company and a Member of Parliament. He was a great friend of the abolitionist William Wilberforce.

TO THE MEMORY OF CHARLES GRANT,
FOR FIFTY YEARS EMPLOYED IN THE CIVIL GOVERNMENT OF INDIA, OR IN DIRECTING ITS AFFAIRS IN ENGLAND;
IN FOUR SUCCESSIVE PARLIAMENTS THE REPRESENTATIVE OF THE COUNTY OF INVERNESS;
WHO, IN THESE HIGH TRUSTS, MANIFESTED A COMMANDING VIGOUR OF UNDERSTANDING AND CHARACTER,
TEMPERED BY CALM JUDGMENT,

St Mary le Strand

STRAND, WC2

The original Strand church was located a short distance to the south of the present site and dedicated to the Nativity of Our Lady and the Innocents. It stood on the land now occupied by Somerset House and in 1549 it was Edward Seymour, the 1st Duke of Somerset, who decided to pull it down to make way for Somerset House. He did promise to rebuild the church but patently thought its stone would be more use for his own construction project and so the parishioners were simply abandoned. They were fortunately able to make the nearby Savoy Chapel their 'temporary' place of worship, but it was actually not until the 'Fifty New Churches Act' of 1710 came into operation that they were able to petition for a new church, and St Mary le Strand was the first to be sanctioned under that new scheme.

The church was built by James Gibbs (1682–1754), a Scottish-born Catholic architect who, as a young man, lost both parents and spent three years wandering around Europe. His final destination was Italy, where he became an architectural student under the guidance of Baroque specialist Carlo Fontana (1638–1714). Although that Italian influence was reflected in many aspects of his church designs, a lot of what he did was a result of his own creativity rather than just mimicking the Italian churches in which he had been trained and educated.

The site chosen for the building of the new Strand church was then occupied by a giant maypole soaring up well over 30m (98ft) high. The custom of maypole dancing had become a popular event and there were many such poles scattered around the City. It was planned to be removed and replaced by a very tall stone replica surmounted by a statue of Queen Anne, deisgned by Gibbs, to serve as a celebration of the most popular monarch, as she was a great lover of royal processions and the Strand churches were set on the regular route from Westminster to St Paul's Cathedral. Sadly, the queen died in 1714 and Gibbs was reluctantly obliged to shelve his plans for the column (his great drawing of it is in the care of the British Museum). So, at that moment he was actually redundant because another architect, Thomas Archer, had been commissioned to build the church and his foundations were already laid. However, the Commissioners started to have doubts, and as Gibbs was free, the building of St Mary le Strand was reallocated to him. That was the good news; the bad news was that he had originally drawn plans for a square church but his predecessor had already laid the base for a rectangular one.

Despite having been obliged to make some alterations to his original plans, Gibbs still managed to introduce some Italianate features, such as the semi-circular portico on the west front. The stage above carries a large central pediment, behind which the spire rises in three stages and is an almost visual replica of St Clement Danes, a design element that is hardly surprising as Gibbs designed and built them both. The exterior combines elegance with drama, and the windowless north and south façades were created to make perfect

---

The elegant Gibbs steeples rising high above the Strand are led by St Mary le Strand with St Clement Danes bringing up the rear. It is fascinating to observe how Gibbs created the effect of soaring church domination, an aspect enhanced by the use of a telephoto lens that visually condenses the subject.

ST MARY LE STRAND 105

backdrops for the colourful royal processions. Sadly, George I and some of the following Hanoverian monarchs were less keen on such public outings – probably because they were significantly less liked than Queen Anne.

The aisleless nave has a most dramatic Gibbs ceiling executed by the wonderfully named Chrysostom Wilkins in 1719, and based upon Rome's churches, one of which was actually designed and built by Gibbs's tutor. The geometrically arranged expanse of squares, triangles and lozenges are tightly packed across the shallow barrel vaulted ceiling, and it is not a prefabricated piece of work. Every single leaf, the tiny flowers and cherubs' faces were all created by hand rather than being pre-formed and just stuck in place.

The Aldwych section of the Strand has been subjected to a major restoration scheme transforming it into a traffic-free zone officially opened in early December 2022. The absolute magic of this project has created a haven of tranquillity and clean air in what was one of London's busier roads. This means that the church can now be safely studied and admired from any angle, and there are copious chairs and tables set around the open spaces. In 1982, St Mary le Strand was designated as the official church of the Women's Royal Naval Service.

OPPOSITE The apse is atmospherically lit with blue glass windows, and at the heart of its dome, directly above the altar, is a gold triangle engraved with the first syllable of the Hebrew name for God surrounded by sunbursts and cherub heads in clouds.

BELOW The semi-circular portico on the west front was definitely an architectural inspiration from the churches Gibbs encountered in Italy, and is best appreciated in winter when the trees are leafless. OVERLEAF The beautifully designed and executed nave roof of St Mary le Strand.

St Martin-in-the-Fields

TRAFALGAR SQUARE, WC2

The first written reference to a church on the site of St Martin's was in the early thirteenth century, and it was later decreed as an independent parish during the reign of Henry VIII in 1542. As its name suggests, St Martin-in-the-Fields really was set in rural countryside and linked to neighbouring communities by basic paths. However, by the eighteenth century, what is now St Martin's Lane had escalated from being simply a footpath into a paved thoroughfare with housing for those upper classes seeking escape from the increasingly overcrowded City of London. The parish church had been patched up, repaired and partially renovated over the decades, but in 1721 it was finally decreed as being structurally dangerous and a new church was commissioned at the behest of George I, who actually went on to become a churchwarden. The architect James Gibbs was commissioned to undertake this new church, and it came at a perfect moment in his burgeoning career, as he had recently completed St Mary le Strand and the steeple of St Clement Danes. Although not lying in an entirely straight line with its predecessors, this third church nevertheless creates an aesthetically beautiful flotilla of Gibbs steeples sailing up the Strand.

His initial plan for a circular design was rejected by the Commissioners, but his alternative of a Greek temple front with a portico on vast columns, straddled by a magnificent 59-m (192-ft) steeple, was accepted. It does seem extraordinary that in the midst of all these projects Gibbs found time to write *A Book of Architecture*, which was published in 1728, and evolved into an almost worldwide 'text book' for church building. The Gibbs steeple/portico formula was adopted by many later English churches, and also in North America and other English-speaking parts of the world.

Given the height of the flights of steps leading up to the portico with its huge Corinthian columns, this early eighteenth-century church must have originally looked somewhat out of place, but all that would change a century later when Trafalgar Square was created. It could well be the most photographed church in London, albeit as simply an appealing background for tourists' photos of lion fountains, or a renowned naval hero called Nelson on a tall column. However, anyone who does actually walk into the church will be instantly captivated by the sheer beauty and creativity of James Gibbs's design and construction.

The pews are dark, but not as dauntingly grim as they might have been during the Victorian era, when box pews were standard because they have now been lowered. The wide nave is flanked by giant columns supporting galleries on three sides, the eastern end housing a royal box furnished with cosy chairs and a fireplace. Queen Mary (1867–1953) was actually the last member of the royal family to regularly worship at St Martin's, the parish church of Buckingham and St James's Palaces and 10 Downing Street. The most visually captivating element of the interior has to be the ceiling, elaborately structured by Gibbs and then lavishly decorated by two Italian artists he specifically commissioned to travel to England for the project.

The 59-m (192-ft) steeple of St Martin-in-the-Field's dominates the 'column corner' of Trafalgar Square and although the neighbouring National Gallery is an imposing piece of work, the beautiful façade and elegant steeple created by James Gibbs (1682–1754) makes his church the architectural champion.

110 GREAT CHURCHES OF LONDON

ST MARTIN-IN-THE-FIELDS 111

St Martin's patron saint is the fourth-century Roman soldier who encountered an almost naked beggar in a raging storm outside the city wall of Amiens in France and instantly slashed his cloak in half to provide at least some protection. That human kindness and care for one's fellow human beings has become the benchmark of St Martin's, an ethos that began to seriously manifest itself during the First World War.

The Reverend Dick Sheppard was vicar of St Martin's from 1914 to 1926, and prior to taking up that post had served as an army chaplain in the trenches of the First World War. That experience had a profound effect, and upon returning he realized that because St Martin's was close to Charing Cross station, it was in the perfect location to offer shelter and comfort to soldiers travelling to and from France. The church and crypt remained open around the clock, providing food and shelter for those in need, a philosophy that has remained in place and significantly expanded into many other areas. That 'ever open door' principle set the pattern for St Martin's continuing pastoral and practical care for the poor, homeless and vulnerable. St Martin's is also renowned for its musical heritage, and in 1958 founded the now internationally famous orchestra, the Academy of St Martin-in-the-Fields.

The view from the nave's gallery towards the west end gives a perfect view of the organ, built by J.W. Walker & Sons in 1990. The symmetry of the pipes is quite mesmerizing and the quality of its casework resulted in it being presented with the Carpenter's Award.

112 GREAT CHURCHES OF LONDON

ABOVE A renewal and restoration programme that began in the first decade of the twenty-first century resulted in far more daylight flooding into the nave. That increase thereby made it easier to view and more fully appreciate the detailed intricacies of the plasterwork.

OPPOSITE The dramatic east window above the altar was the final addition of the church's restoration programme. The abstract cross was created by Shirazeh Houshiary and Pip Horne, emphasizing Gibbs's original desire for the church to be filled with light and not darkened by excessive coloured glass.

114 GREAT CHURCHES OF LONDON

ABOVE The pulpit may not be the original one, but is nevertheless a beautiful piece of carved woodwork, perfectly reflecting the style and artistry of its predecessor. It is now repositioned closer to its former location in order to generate a greater communication with the congregation.

The captivating east window and chandeliers draw one's attention up to the beautiful nave ceiling. It was created by the Italian artists Giuseppe Artari and Giovanni Bagutti, whose amazing craftsmanship impressed Gibbs, and he lauded them as the best ornamentists to have ever arrived in England.

St George's

HANOVER SQUARE, W1

As the City of London's traders and labourers sought to live as close as possible to their workplaces, the gentry and nobility moved further west to escape the overcrowding; Hanover Square was one of the first such affluent areas to be established. Its name originated from the new royal dynasty that began its protracted reigns with the accession of George I in 1714. As the population increased in certain areas, so did the need for churches, and the parishioners of this smart new suburb duly applied the Commission for Building Fifty New Churches. Their request was approved and the architect John James (1673–1746) was chosen to build the new church on what was actually quite a small plot of land donated by a local resident. The contract duly stipulated that the design should be modified to ensure that the cost would not exceed £10,000 (currently approximately £2.25 million).

John James began his career serving under Sir Christopher Wren, and then gradually increased his own standing within the architectural community. His submitted plans for St George's were actually deemed more appropriate than those proposed by James Gibbs, the acclaimed architect of St Mary le Strand and St Martin-in-the-Fields. The first stone was laid in February 1721 by the site's donor, General William Stewart, and completed four years later in 1725. The four differing sides of St George's perfectly illustrate just what practical and design challenges architects had to overcome when presented with a piece of land by a well-intentioned but non-architecturally minded donor. This is particularly well illustrated if approaching the church via Maddox Street, a road that suddenly halves in width as it squeezes past the east and north aspects of the church. As one then arrives at St George's west end, the contrast could not be more spectacularly different, and the church's façade is a really impressively designed and brilliantly executed piece of Classical architecture.

John James created a six-columned Corinthian portico that actually extends into the road by straddling the pavement and, consequently, pedestrians still have to cope with ascending and descending two flights of steps. The views from Hanover Square and St George Street really are most aesthetically impressive, and even though some architectural historians have not over-enthused about the tower, it has a most appropriate size and design that perfectly complements the dramatic portico.

The interior has north- and south-facing galleries supported by square pillars that transform into Corinthian columns with gilded capitals. The galleries curve round to flank the organ set on the west end, and although there is a formal aura attached to the church's interior layout and furnishings, it adheres perfectly to the ideology once proclaimed by Christopher Wren that audibility and visibility were supremely important. Interestingly enough, those facets were actually enhanced during the Victorian era, a time when many churches were being somewhat over-formalized. The box pews were remodelled and reduced in height, and a similar approach was also given to the pulpit, thereby enabling the priest to be more at one with the congregation rather than formally 'lecturing'.

The view from the organ loft shows the Victorian black and white chancel floor and choir stalls backed by the altar, reredos and beautiful sixteenth-century stained glass window. The winter services are very atmospheric when all of the interior is lit by the massive chandeliers.

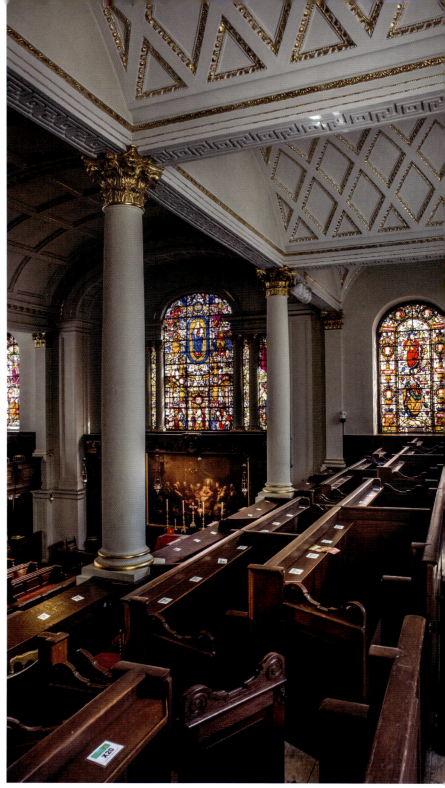

Those late nineteenth-century refurbishments also resulted in the creation of a chancel with a black and white marble floor and choir stalls, thereby bringing the choristers down from the west gallery into a more inclusive location.

St George's is renowned for its music and has a professional choir, maintaining the church's links to the highest standards, as one of its regular parishioners was the German composer George Frideric Handel (1685–1759). He actually lived close by in Brook Street on the edge of Hanover Square, and it was there that he composed the *Messiah* and several other notable works. In a curious musical coincidence, albeit spread centuries apart, the house next door to the Handel residence was where Jimi Hendrix lived, and those two houses have now been converted into the Handel Hendrix House.

The body of the church may only date back to the early eighteenth century, but one of its finest works of art is much older. The glass windows of the east end above the altar were actually made around 1525 by Arnold of Nijmegen for a Carmelite church in Antwerp, Belgium, and were somehow acquired in the early nineteenth century. Although designed for tall Gothic windows, the glass was nevertheless successfully edited to fit into its new home and St George's ranks highly on the list of churches built on the Coal Tax that funded the Fifty New Churches campaign.

OPPOSITE: TOP LEFT The corner column and decorated capital supporting the front portico. TOP RIGHT St George's 'dress circle' of elegantly carved pews. BOTTOM LEFT Virgin and Child in the heart of the sixteenth-century altar window. BOTTOM RIGHT The font is made from carved and lightly veined marble.

ABOVE A view of the church from St George Street highlighting the dramatic portico thrusting right out onto the road's edge. OVERLEAF Columns and wood carvings in the Grinling Gibbons style frame the altar's beautiful artwork, a painting of the Last Supper by William Kent (1684–1748).

St Paul's

DEPTFORD, SE8

Deptford lies on the south bank of the River Thames some six miles east of London and next door to Greenwich. Its riverside location made Deptford an important centre for both naval and trade shipping, with the first Royal Naval Dockyard being established there by Henry VIII in 1513. Having originally been two separate communities, Deptford's continuing success in the shipping industry resulted in a significant expansion into one large and thriving community. That increase in population meant that its existing churches were struggling to cope and consequently an application for a new church was submitted to the Fifty New Churches Commission. Permission was duly granted and that assignment was handed to Thomas Archer (c.1668–1745), who in 1711 had been appointed as a Commissioner in the Fifty New Churches organization. Work began a year later and although much of the church was actually constructed by 1720, craftsmen were fully occupied for a further decade and its consecration did not happen until June 1730.

Archer was the son of a Warwickshire squire, educated at Trinity College, Oxford, and then spent time travelling in Europe. For many years, records of his adventures went undiscovered until a stash of small notebooks was uncovered in an archive of files in Stratford-upon-Avon. The notes and drawings in those books confirmed that he was seriously impassioned by the architecture of Europe, spending time in Belgium and Holland before ending his travels in Rome. His definite Italian influences in the sphere of church building could certainly be attributed to architects such as Bernini and Borromini, whose interior and exterior designs led them to be celebrated as two significant figures in the progression of Baroque architecture.

St Paul's is actually not a vast church, but that is the initial impression one gets when approaching on foot due to the absolute solidity and size of the four massive Tuscan columns supporting the semi-circular portico. A raised crypt enhances the impression of size and majesty as the main body of the church is therefore significantly raised and entered via a flight of steps. The slender tower and spire rising high above the portico create a perfectly symmetrical and aesthetic combination, and St Paul's has been praised as one of London's finest Baroque churches. Some critics did suggest that the portico and columns were influenced by elements of Wren's St Paul's Cathedral, but the reality was that Archer's design was most probably derived from Santa Maria della Pace in Rome.

The church's east end mirrors the main façade and comprises a smaller portico, and both north and south sides are symmetrically matched with elegant double staircases. Every design and structural aspect of the church is enhanced by the use of Portland stone, a building material that has been quarried for centuries on the rocky peninsula of Portland, just off the Dorset coast. Over six million tonnes of stone from these quarries was used in the rebuilding of around fifty churches and other buildings after the Great Fire of London. It was fortunate that London is directly linked to the sea via

---

St Paul's is a Baroque architectural masterpiece that is well worth making the 10-km (6-mile) journey from Central London to appreciate. The surrounding trees have grown so much that Thomas Archer's design is being increasingly hidden, but there is a good view from the train station's elevated platform.

124 GREAT CHURCHES OF LONDON

the River Thames, as one cannot imagine that quantity of stone being trundled by horse and cart over rough tracks.

The church interior is virtually a square with side aisles, each separated by two Corinthian columns, and an organ gallery is set above the main entrance. There is a most elegant Venetian east window that curves around the apse, and the walls are adorned with many memorials, the most significant being the two rose windows dedicated to Canon David Diamond. Church rectors can become important members of the wider community outside the church walls, and St Paul's was immensely fortunate to have had him from 1969 until his sudden death in 1992. Deptford had become a run-down place through the demise of its maritime-related industries, and St Paul's was a dilapidated church with a handful of parishioners on the verge of closure. Consequently, he thought that the Church should lead in picking up the fragments of a crumbling society. His quite remarkable ministry resulted in the restoration of St Paul's, the establishment of the famous Deptford Festival, and so many other things that really brought the community back together in so many ways. Had it not been for those relentless efforts, we might not still have this Baroque architectural jewel to admire. It could actually be even better admired if the encroaching trees could be pruned back a little.

ABOVE The western end of St Paul's is a symmetrical masterpiece, enhanced by being on a raised platform with triple flights of steps. It is not until one actually climbs up to the four Tuscan columns that their sheer size is fully appreciated.

RIGHT After a fire in 2000, the church was redecorated back to its original interior design, and plain glass has replaced the stained glass in a Venetian window that curves round the apse and then fits into a screen terminating in a column at each end.

LATER GEORGIAN

WESLEY'S CHAPEL

CITY ROAD, EC1

An evocative bronze statue of John Wesley with prayer book in hand stands on a marble plinth set in front of the Methodist Chapel that was opened in 1778. Although places of worship referred to as chapels are generally smaller than churches, there is nothing diminutive about this one, which truly reflects its stature as the mother church of Methodism. Wesley's Chapel façade comprises five bays, the middle three of which project slightly and are topped by a quite dramatic portal flanked by fluted columns. Above is a line of large first-floor windows that flood the upper gallery with copious amounts of daylight. The chapel stands towards the rear of a large cobbled courtyard that also contains the Georgian house built for Wesley just a year after the chapel opened, and it was there that he passed away in 1791.

Wesley was the son of an Anglican parson and born in the rural Lincolnshire village of Epworth in 1703. He was educated at London's Charterhouse School and Christ Church College at Oxford University, and was later ordained into the Church of England.

His younger brother Charles, born just four years later, would also become heavily involved in the spread of Methodism throughout Britain and became renowned as a prolific hymn writer. The principles Wesley adhered to were finding a new way to worship that connected with the increasing numbers of poor people in eighteenth-century Britain. The foundation of the Wesleyan movement coincided with an emergence of evangelical spiritual renewal throughout Europe. It was being realized that many people's needs were simply not being met and that the Church was offering little or no help in that respect.

Although Wesley spent a lot of time travelling around the country to preach in both churches and public spaces, he also created the Foundery Chapel that was in use 1739–78 in a disused armaments factory, located just a short distance away from the one seen here. It was more than just a place for preaching and included a dispensary and a small school to provide medication and education for the increasing numbers of poverty-stricken people in a burgeoning industrial era. When the Foundery's lease expired, Wesley commissioned the architect George Dance the Younger to design and create the new chapel that was completed in 1778. In a curious coincidence, George Dance (1741–1825) was actually buried in St Paul's Cathedral and it was from there that loads of surplus firm soil had earlier been acquired to bolster the soft ground on which the Wesley Chapel was being built.

Directly across the road from Wesley's Chapel is the Bunhill Fields burial site. It is a most atmospheric location, now cared for by the City of London Corporation, and one of its many gravestones is that of Susanna Wesley, the mother of John and Charles. Due to it being outside the City and not attached to a particular church, it was used as a significant burial ground for Nonconformists. Several famous literary and artistic figures including William Blake, John Bunyan and Daniel Defoe have memorials there.

The Wesley statue was sculpted by John Adams-Acton in 1891 and set upon a plinth in front of the chapel inscribed with the words 'The World is My Parish'. Methodism had indeed evolved into a worldwide religion with a very significant uptake in the United States of America. PREVIOUS PAGES Greenwich Hospital Chapel.

Wesley's Chapel 131

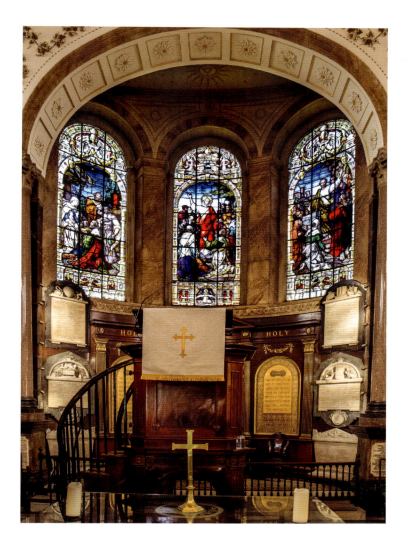

There are actually two chapels housed within the new building, the main one of which has the proportions of a church. The upper galleries extend significantly outwards into the nave's centre, and although now supported by beautiful Jasper columns, their security was originally ensured by wooden sailing ship masts donated by George III. The layout and dimensions of the interior could be deemed more 'standard' church than Nonconformist, but one feature totally 'Wesleyfied' is the pulpit. The one standing there today is visually impressive but lacks the dominating aura its predecessor must have possessed. It was a significantly higher triple-decker and, whether sat in the nave or galleries, there was no hiding place for any members of the congregation. That was apparently demonstrated during Wesley's first sermon in 1778 as he verbally lambasted the fashionable 'Sunday-best' hats of the startled congregation, citing the alleged dangers of affluence.

The smaller place of worship is the Foundery Chapel, named after the original one just up the road, and furnished with some of its pews and benches. It also houses the small organ played by Charles Wesley while creating his vast portfolio of hymns.

Escalating structural issues threatened the very existence of the chapel but, following a worldwide fund-raising operation, it was substantially restored during the 1970s and now has an informative museum in the crypt. In 1978, exactly 200 years since the chapel opened, there was a reopening ceremony attended by Queen Elizabeth II.

OPPOSITE The Wesley Chapel interior was transformed during a late nineteenth-century restoration and has lost its sense of austerity somewhat, but is nevertheless still visually appealing. The gallery is now raked and the east end windows are filled with richly coloured stained glass.

ABOVE LEFT The pulpit and east end with altar and communion railings that were donated by Margaret Thatcher, who was married here in 1951; her children, Mark and Carol, were also baptized in the chapel. ABOVE RIGHT The tiny Foundery Chapel is an intimate place for quiet contemplation.

Greenwich Hospital Chapel

GREENWICH, SE10

Greenwich may not be on the doorstep of Central London but road, rail and river access is very easy. My favourite method is via the express boat services that have many access points along the Thames and deliver passengers right to the doorstep of this glorious architectural gem that has been rightly classed a UNESCO World Heritage Site. However, regardless of which mode of transport one employs, it really is worth making a pilgrimage via the Greenwich Foot Tunnel to the Island Gardens set directly across the river. It is only from there that one actually gets to see the beautiful symmetry of the Old Royal Naval College, originally created as a hospital at the behest of Queen Mary during her joint reign with William of Orange in the final decade of the seventeenth century. Appalled by witnessing the injuries inflicted upon English sailors in conflicts with the French, she wished to establish a hospital for wounded, disabled and elderly sailors similar to the Royal Military Hospital in Chelsea. The Queen's choice of location maintained an association between Greenwich and the Navy that extended back to the Tudor period, and Sir Christopher Wren volunteered to design the hospital free of charge.

Although planned differently at the outset, the great hospital ended up as two perfectly symmetrical sections after Queen Mary insisted that her view of the Thames from the already established Queen's House should not be obstructed. The Queen Mary Block on the east side of the development is the one that includes the chapel, and its domed tower stands over the entrance. Fate could have easily affected the outcome of this project because Mary died from smallpox in 1694 at the age of just thirty-two years. Despite being utterly devastated by her untimely death, William vowed to honour what she had described as 'the darling project of my life'. The hospital partially opened in 1705 with just forty-five injured and disabled naval seamen living there but, due to rising costs and structural issues, it took many years to actually progress towards absolute completion. Celebrated architects such as Hawksmoor and Vanbrugh contributed their own artistry to the hospital project that was eventually finished by Thomas Ripley in 1752. However, the chapel itself did not fare so well, and Wren's work was consumed by a bad fire in 1779 and subsequently rebuilt by James 'Athenian' Stuart (1713–88) and his hugely talented Clerk of Works, William Newton.

Stuart's Grecian-flavoured nickname related to him being widely recognized for his role in pioneering Neoclassicism. He spent several years studying in Greece and had become widely known through publishing several volumes of *Antiquities of Athens*, books that helped shape the European understanding of Ancient Greece. The exterior of the chapel is architecturally and visually impressive and, unusually for a galleried church, actually comprises three sets of windows, with the lower one illuminating the crypt. Entry into the chapel is via an octagonal vestibule, one wall of which contains a moving monument to the famed Arctic explorer Sir John Franklin and a crew of 129 men in two ships who all perished in their quest for a final

---

Sir Christopher Wren's design for the Royal Hospital split the site into four quadrants, with the King William Court and the Queen Mary Court being the two set further back from the river and topped with large domes. The hospital was created in the Queen Mary Block.

134 Great Churches of London

GREENWICH HOSPITAL CHAPEL   135

stretch of the Northwest Passage that would link the Pacific and Atlantic oceans.

As a flight of steps leads up into the chapel, the walls are adorned with four large statues representing Faith, Hope, Charity and Meekness, all created by the American artist Benjamin West (1738–1820) from Coade stone, a material named after its eighteenth-century inventor, Eleanor Coade (1733–1821). West was also responsible for the large painting dominating the chapel's east end that appropriately features St Paul being saved from a shipwreck in Malta. That Mediterranean island was probably only too well known by the many sailors who attended services in the chapel. Two pairs of large Corinthian columns stand either side of the altar, something else in the chapel made from Coade stone, a tough, hardwearing artificial 'stone' that was actually a ceramic – being a mix of terracotta, silicates and glass fired for four days in a very hot kiln that enabled fine detailed decoration in a manner that actual stone would not.

The decor throughout the chapel is a visually captivating blend of Neoclassic and naval designs featuring anchors, mermaids and mermen, all entwined by twisted ropes, and resting close by pieces of artwork associated more with ancient Athens rather than England. The chapel underwent a major restoration during the 1950s, with much of the colour being returned to its original form, and remains an architectural and artistic masterpiece.

The interior of the Chapel of St Peter and St Paul is a Neoclassical masterpiece created by James Stewart and William Newton. The narrow galleries and gently curved ceiling help create perfect acoustics for both hymns and concert music. OVERLEAF The immaculately carved pulpit, gallery supports and organ loft.

GREENWICH HOSPITAL CHAPEL 139

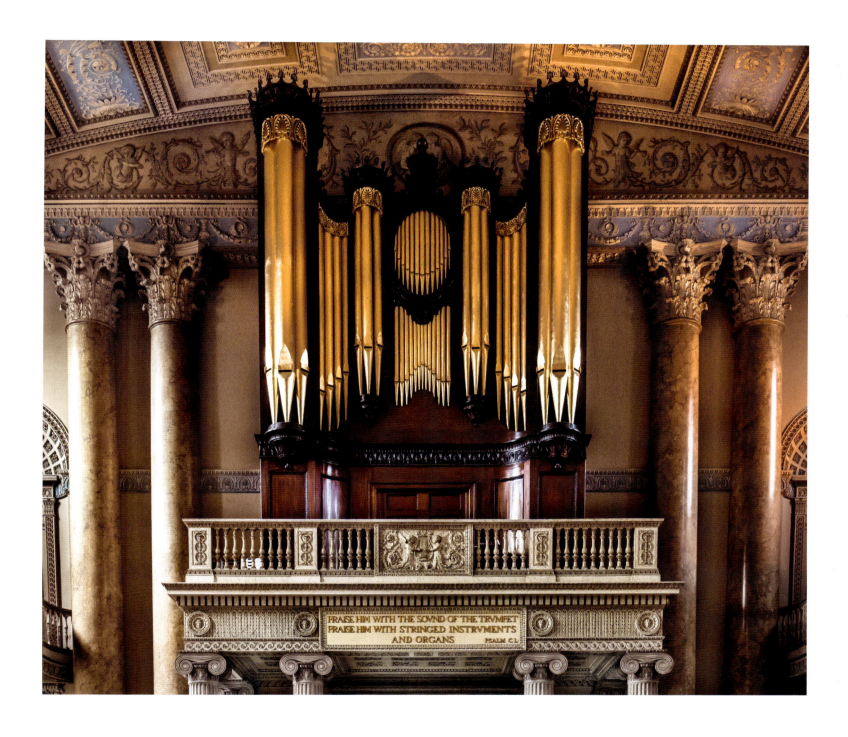

OPPOSITE: ABOVE The ceiling was designed by master plasterer John Papworth in a Neoclassical design of squares and octagons, and the intricate central ornaments were actually carved, rather than cast in moulds. BELOW The semi-circular altar was created from gilded Coade stone angels and a marble top.

ABOVE The organ was made by the leading eighteenth-century organ builder, Samuel Green. It is probably the largest instrument built by him still in its original position and has a case of Spanish mahogany. The original pipework noted for its purity of tone is still in use.

St Pancras New Church

EUSTON ROAD, NW1

Two London churches, a road and railway station all share the name of St Pancras. A fourteen-year-old boy born in what is now Turkey had lost both parents and went to live with his uncle in Rome, where they both converted to Christianity. In 304 CE he was in a group of Christians rounded up and brought before the authorities to renounce their faith and offer sacrifices to the Roman gods. The Emperor Diocletian was impressed with the boy's dedication and gave further chances for him to conform, but Pancras refused and on 12 May was beheaded on the Via Aurelia outside Rome.

The older of the two St Pancras churches dates back to Medieval times and centuries ago was set in what was then open countryside. As London expanded outwards from the City, that village church with a maximum capacity of 150 people was deemed unsuitable, and so in 1816 an Act of Parliament authorized the building of a new church to serve the rapidly increasing population around Euston Square's development.

The authorities held a design competition for the new church and the winners were the Inwood family partnership comprising William Inwood and his elder son Henry William, who was actually studying Hellenic architecture in Athens when the news of their victory was announced. He had been researching the Classical buildings and making plaster casts of some important details on a distinctive Acropolis temple called the Erechtheion, and the other building used as a significant point of reference was the Tower of the Winds.

The most eye-catching elements on the exterior of St Pancras are the caryatids, the draped female figures generally used as decorative columns to support a building's entablature. However, unlike the Athenian originals upon which they were based, these are actually bearing water jugs and torches, symbols that referred to the presence of death. They are standing in groups of four over both entrances to the church's crypt, once used for burials but now converted into an atmospheric art and exhibition centre. The figures were made from a combination of robust Coade stone set around columns of Portland stone that were themselves strengthened by internal iron bars. The caryatids were created by the sculptor J.C.F. Rossi, who had previously worked at the South London Coade factory and was responsible for many works of art with this durable and versatile man-made material on both public and private buildings. These graphic statues from Ancient Greece staring expressionlessly at the never-ending streams of taxis and buses ploughing up and down Euston Road are definitely St Pancras' unique architectural feature.

However, it is at the west end that the Inwoods really presented their understanding of Ancient Greek architecture. They created a dramatic façade for the church with a substantial six-column Ionic portico and a tower based upon the Tower of the Winds, with three diminishing-sized octagons rising up to a short obelisk spire and cross. It really is an impressive piece of architecture that must have created a huge amount of interest from parishioners and passers-by who

---

Although appearing to be simply decorative sculpted figures, the role of the Ancient Greek caryatids was to not only adorn but support the entablature of a building. The St Pancras ones were modelled on those created for the Erechtheion, set high on the Acropolis in Athens.

may not have had any prior knowledge or awareness of Ancient Greece.

The main entrance into the church is through a huge red doorway surrounded by elaborate mouldings and rosettes, all of which are still remarkably crisp and not weathered in the same manner as much of the other Portland stone used for the exterior stone work. This is due to that fact that they were made from 'fake' stone created from crushed limestone and cement and then moulded into shape. The doorway leads into the church past another half dozen ionic columns supporting the organ loft, and one then stands in the vast galleried arena that is the main body of the church. The most eye-catching feature is the way in which the east end apse was created using a raised platform that bears the six columns whose bases and capitals were exact replicas of those on the Erechtheion noted by Henry Inwood on his research trip to Athens.

The columns themselves were actually constructed from scagliola, a form of synthetic stone developed in Italy during the seventeenth century which, by two centuries later, had become an almost worldwide, affordable stone substitute for such demanding projects. The foundation stone was laid by the Duke of York in 1819 and construction completed just three years later. The church of St Pancras was the first Greek Revival church built in London, and was also the most expensive since the rebuilding of St Paul's Cathedral.

ABOVE The east end of the church has a semi-circular apse surmounted by six columns, the bases and capitals of which were copied from the Erectheion in Athens. The columns are not stone but clever fakes imitating the appearance of a precious Greek stone known as Verde Antico.

ST PANCRAS NEW CHURCH 143

ABOVE The pulpit is the original one created in 1822, with wood from the famous ancient oak tree in Hainault Forest, which had blown down a couple of years earlier. The oak was ancient and famous enough to have a country fair named after it, and a pub has also been christened with that name. The line of columns that support the wide gallery run close by the pulpit, and when one contemplates that the church could accommodate 2,500 worshippers, how did the vicar's voice manage to penetrate every corner in those pre-technology days?

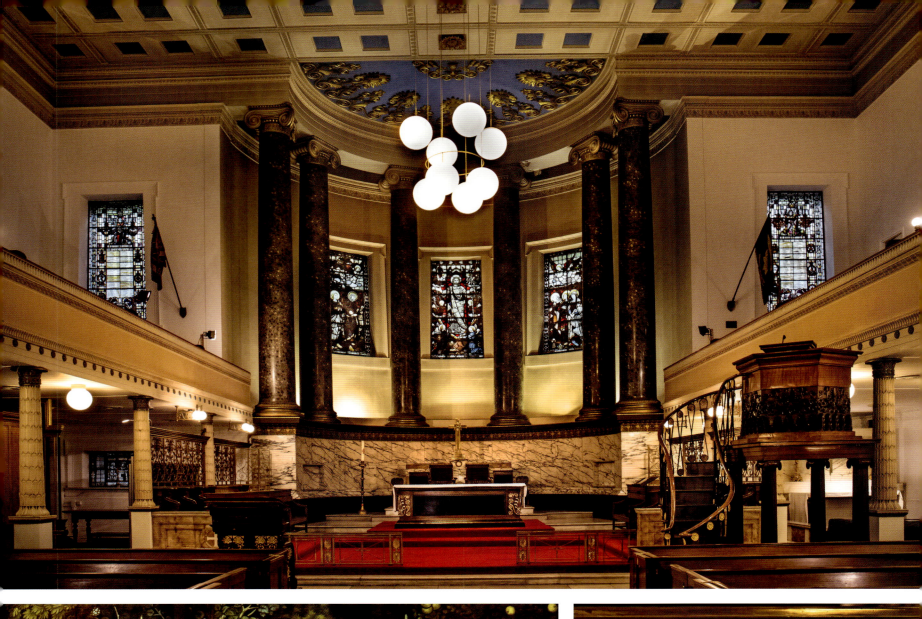

TO THE GLORY OF GOD
PRESENTED BY H REGNART AD 1881

ST PANCRAS NEW CHURCH 145

OPPOSITE: TOP The perfect symmetry of St Pancras viewed from the west entrance. BOTTOM LEFT Alterations and updates during the Victorian era included the addition of stained glass, most of which was by the legendary studio of Clayton & Bell. BOTTOM RIGHT The communion rail.

ABOVE The west front with its Ionic columns and tower comprising three diminishing-sized octagons based on the Tower of the Winds. Even though this photograph was taken directly into the rising sun, I got light rather than shadow courtesy of a glass-fronted building behind, which acted as a mirror.

St Mary's

PADDINGTON GREEN, W2

As the Westway flyover bearing one of the capital's main arterial routes descends to ground level en route to Paddington, Edgware and the centre of London, drivers may be watching for brake lights rather than admiring the church of St Mary standing quite close to the road network. Historical documents show that Paddington's first parish church established during the fourteenth century was erected to the north of the current site. Records covering the following centuries were somewhat vague, however, there is confirmation that the original church dedicated to St Nicholas was demolished and rebuilt during the latter part of the seventeenth century. That successor apparently had a comparatively short life due to structural defects, and so an Act of Parliament, passed in 1789, authorized the building of a new, larger Paddington parish church on nearby land donated by the Bishop of London.

Architect John Plaw (1745–1820) was then commissioned to design and build the new church and he created a brick structure in the form of a Greek Cross that was consecrated in 1791. That style comprises a square format with equal-length arms projecting from each side, a shallow white dome supported by matching columns and semi-circular porches created from Portland stone. The south-facing arm is the main entrance and as such was enhanced with more elaborate decoration than the building's other façades. As one enters through that portal into the main body of the church, the sense of perfect symmetry is enhanced by the square format, Doric- and Corinthian-style columns, softly coloured box pews and an upper gallery extending around three sides. St Mary's is actually rather like a small, intimate theatre with reversed seating categories whereby the stalls are up in the dress circle and the expensive boxes are set on the ground floor directly in front of the stage. That sense of close community is also enhanced by the large, beautifully carved pulpit closely integrated into the rows of boxed pews. The most striking view is towards the chancel, where a large Venetian window frames the altar and both chancel walls are adorned with an impressive array of memorial plaques.

Having been enlarged six times during the course of the eighteenth and nineteenth centuries, St Mary's had become one of the largest churchyards in London, and during the latter years of the eighteenth century became a popular place to be buried by those not even from the parish. At that time, Paddington Green still had the charm of a countryside village and members of London Society requested interment there rather than in the City. However, as time passed, London really started expanding and from the mid-nineteenth century onwards Paddington's population grew from around 2,000 to well over 20,000. This was due to both industrial growth and the arrival of railways as a new mode of public transport, and the building of Paddington's rail terminus. It was therefore in 1845 that St Mary's was deemed inadequate to serve its increasingly large population and the status of parish church was transferred to the newly built church of St

---

St Mary's is a beautiful church, and the fact that it has survived the onslaught of road building into the heart of London is a tribute to those who defended its heritage, and is doubly precious being a rare example of a church built in the Greek Cross style.

James set just a few streets away from the station. However, St Mary's continued to care for the local community and its extensive churchyard was still chosen as a final resting place for both locals and some well-known personalities, the most significant being the famous actress Sarah Siddons (1755–1831). Her original tomb lies way out in the churchyard but is also remembered by an imposing statue set in a garden adjacent to the church. Unveiled in 1897, it had been created by French sculptor Léon-Joseph Chavalliaud and was based upon the painting *Mrs Siddons as the Tragic Muse* by Sir Joshua Reynolds.

Standing inside St Mary's admiring the immaculate decor and furnishings, one might ponder on how well everything has survived over time, but in reality, the previously 'Victorianized' church was only renovated back to much of its late eighteenth-century layout in 1972. The vicar during that period, the Reverend John Foster, had discovered that financial compensation paid by the London County Council for the construction of the Harrow Road flyover over part of the church's land had been misdirected and was consequently reclaimed. That reimbursement enabled St Mary's to be reverted back to its original glory, and the architect in charge of that project was Raymond Erith, who also designed the exquisite central chandelier. Upon completion, the subsequent service of Thanksgiving was attended by Queen Elizabeth, the Queen Mother, the Bishop of London and Lord Mayor of Westminster.

The interior of St Mary's is an immaculate portrait of how the church must have originally appeared to its late eighteenth-century parishioners, and one almost senses that the only difference between then and the present day is that the chandeliers are now powered by electricity rather than candles!

ST MARY'S 151

OPPOSITE The chancel may be smaller than others but its layout and atmosphere are just perfect. The walls are adorned with a variety of memorials, many of which relate to those from central London who had decided that they would rather be buried in 'rural' Paddington.

ABOVE The wide expanses of St Mary's churchyard are dotted with its original tombs and gravestones. One of the most famous people interred there was the legendary nineteenth-century actress Sarah Siddons, who is also remembered by a beautifully sculpted statue closer to the church.

ALL SOULS

LANGHAM PLACE, W1

The much-revered architect John Nash (1752–1835), who designed and built All Souls, was also creator of significant areas in the heart of London, some portions of which have survived to the present day. His most prolific buildings were erected around the beautiful area of Regent's Park, parts of which are still adorned by his Grade I-listed terraces. Many of those schemes that went on to shape central London in terms of both architecture and road layout were planned and completed by Nash during a close association with the Prince Regent (r. 1811–20), who became King George IV (r. 1820–30). One of his first major commissions was the design and development of an area extending from St James's Park up Regent Street, past what is now Oxford Circus and northwards to Regent's Park. Aesthetically, there were occasional layout issues caused by tenacious landowners who refused to part with their precious parcels of land. Nash was therefore obliged to amend his symmetry and make a swerve to the left, and it was on that bend that he placed the distinctive church of All Souls that now has the vast BBC building rising up behind it. For the post-Second World War era it became extremely convenient for the BBC to have a real church with excellent acoustics on its doorstep, and so spanning around four decades from 1951 onwards, the BBC Radio's Daily Service was broadcast live from All Souls, albeit with occasional hints of pneumatic drilling from roadworks as a background effect.

Although a significant portion of Nash's work was at the king's behest, the design and construction of All Souls was actually a Commissioner's Church and was built between 1822 and 1824. Due to factors such as the Industrial Revolution, the rapidly growing population of Britain was becoming ever more concentrated into urban areas, and there were simply not enough churches to support them. Around the end of the eighteenth century, the St Marylebone district of London (including the Regent Street and Regent's Park areas) had just under 9,000 church seats for a population that had increased to 76,000. Most of the suburban churches were constructed in basic architectural styles to simply cater for larger congregations, but those in the more affluent areas around the heart of London were in a far more creative style that would appeal to their higher status parishioners. There were almost 150 new churches built under this scheme, funded mostly by the Government.

The design of All Souls was extremely clever as it was given a 290-degree circular portico of Grecian pillars with a similarly decorated tower topped with an almost needle-thin spire. Consequently, regardless of whether one viewed the church from Regent Street or Portland Place, that design overcame the church's 'dog-leg' location and it looked the same from almost every angle. For some reason, the fact that Nash had topped his elegant Grecian-pillared portico and tower with a sharp needle was regarded in some quarters as an architectural insult and he was somewhat childishly lambasted in both the press and Parliament.

The west end gallery is dominated by the magnificent organ set in a casing of Spanish mahogany designed by Nash. It was originally built in 1913, dismantled for safety during the Second World War and then rebuilt twice again in 1951 and 1976. The gallery bears King George IV's coat of arms.

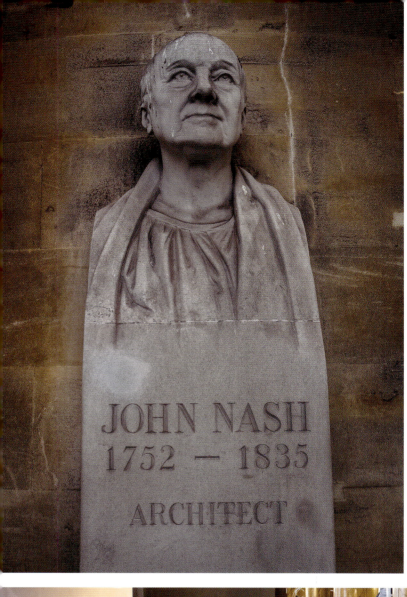

ALL SOULS 155

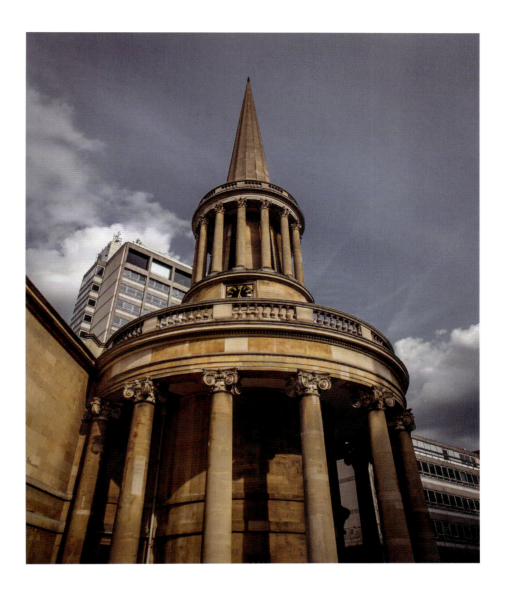

The Grecian theme extends into the interior where three sides of the nave have galleries supported by gilded false-marble columns and just about every surface is adorned by classical decoration. All Souls' equivalent to a chancel is a raised section flanked by more golden pillars, and its equivalent to a reredos is the beautiful painting of Christ created by the much-acclaimed Victorian artist Richard Westall. It was donated by George IV in gratitude for the new Regent Street created by Nash that successfully linked the royal residence of Carlton House set on The Mall up to Regent's Park. In common with so many other churches in London, All Souls did not escape unscathed during the Second World War and its roof and spire were quite badly damaged in 1940. Instability caused by the explosion meant that the church could not be reoccupied until 1951, a year after the appointment of John Stott as rector. He remained in that post for the next twenty-five years and, through those two and a half decades, All Souls thrived and grew as a serious Evangelical church that still remains focused on support and help for all ages of the community. This is not just a parish church looking after parishioners from the surrounding streets; its umbrella of help, care and guidance now spreads so much wider than its famous niche next to the BBC.

OPPOSITE: TOP LEFT The 1956 bust of John Nash set in the portico. TOP RIGHT One of the richly carved capitals on a portico column. BOTTOM One of the upper galleries.

ABOVE The elegantly created façade of All Souls with its Grecian-style portico and tower topped with a needle-sharp spire.

VICTORIAN AND EDWARDIAN

All Saints

MARGARET STREET, W1

Margaret Street begins at the northern end of Regent Street and then runs eastwards and parallel to Oxford Street. It is lined with buildings created from a variety of materials, predominantly brick or pale stone. Towards its eastern end there is suddenly an enclave of three red and black brick structures, one of which is a church created in the hallmark design of the acclaimed nineteenth-century architect William Butterfield (1814–1900). The other two buildings, on what was a rather cramped site of about 9m² (100 sq. ft), were a choir school and vicarage. London architects were frequently burdened with the task of creating places of worship in difficult locations, usually because patches of land donated by sponsors were already tightly flanked by buildings in different ownership. In the case of All Saints, it had been commissioned by the High Church devotee Alexander Beresford-Hope MP and built on a site occupied since 1760 by the Margaret Chapel, which had become an oasis for supporters of the Anglo-Catholic movement since 1839. That group also became known as the Oxford Movement, due to the fact that most of its innovators were closely associated with the university. Cambridge was another major university hosting a similar group established to revive and promote medieval church architecture. It became based in London during the mid-1840s and renamed as the Ecclesiological Movement. From that period onwards, those Oxford and Cambridge groups, which included high-ranking members of both the Anglican Church and Parliament, strived to steer church architecture and ritual back to the Medieval Gothic periods. Although the Victorian era was regarded as rather dour in some respects, the Anglo-Catholics sought to elevate that mid-nineteenth-century approach from tedious (their words) back to the High Church ritual.

All Saints was built between 1849 and 1859, and Butterfield produced one of the first great examples of High Church Gothic Revivalism that was passionately conceived, properly planned and well constructed. The selected architectural style was based upon thirteenth-century Gothic, with an easily visible chancel giving upwards progression towards the altar. Beresford-Hope was seeking an almost theatrical environment with space for processions, services illuminated by copious candlelight and an almost ritualistic veneration of saints.

The trio of buildings are readily landmarked from a distance by the church's sharp pointed spire rising to a height of 69m (226ft), but the main body of the church is set back from the road with its two companions taking closer order on Margaret Street. The exterior was a fascinating compilation of building materials and tones but, as soon as one walks through the delightful courtyard and into the church, there is scarcely a trace of plain stone or brick. The walls of All Saints are a remarkable palette of images and colour. The only visible sign of natural stone emanates

---

Despite standing discreetly in a non-prominent location to the north of Oxford Street, All Saints is nevertheless lauded as one of England's most celebrated Victorian churches in the portfolio of the burgeoning Anglo-Catholic movement. The chancel, altar and reredos are framed by beautiful paintings from Sir Ninian Comper. PREVIOUS PAGES St Cuthbert's, Philbeach Gardens.

160 Great Churches of London

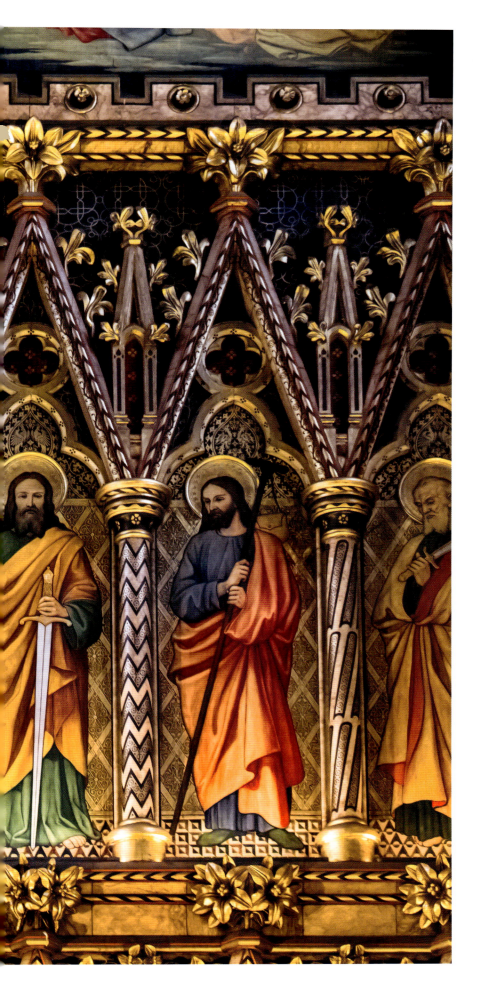

from the columns and arches dividing the nave with the north and south chapels, and those true marble colours include red Languedoc, yellow Sienna and green Connemara.

It actually takes a little time for one's eyes to settle on any particular area, as all the richly coloured features are impressively captivating.

After that first moment, one's focus is invariably towards the east end and its seriously High Church layout, design and artwork. This is accentuated by the fact that the nave is little more than two bays long and the decorative majesty of the chancel projects itself into a substantial portion of the church. It is also about elevation of the altar, and that commences with two steps up to a marble rail dividing the nave and chancel. After the choir, three further steps lead up to the sanctuary and a final two ascend to the altar. That significant ascension up to the church's focal point under flickering candlelight must have been an impressive sight for worshippers sat in the nave, and a particularly humbling but rewarding experience for the choristers and clergy enveloped in that three-sided palette of colour and atmosphere. The original painted panels of the reredos were executed by William Dyce but later renewed by Sir John Ninian Comper in 1909, who also created the sanctuary's side panels five years later. He was responsible for the late Gothic-style Lady Chapel, several other parts of the church's elaborate decor, and also designed the silver pyx (Blessed Sacrament holder) suspended over the altar. Every square inch of this church was successfully designed and created to meet the needs of High Church ritual and is probably William Butterfield's finest piece of religious architecture.

Comper's painted reredos panels completed in 1909 are faithful copies of the originals. The lower central panel depicts the Nativity and the second row is a magnificent portrayal of the Crucifixion with Jesus flanked on either side of the Cross by the Apostles.

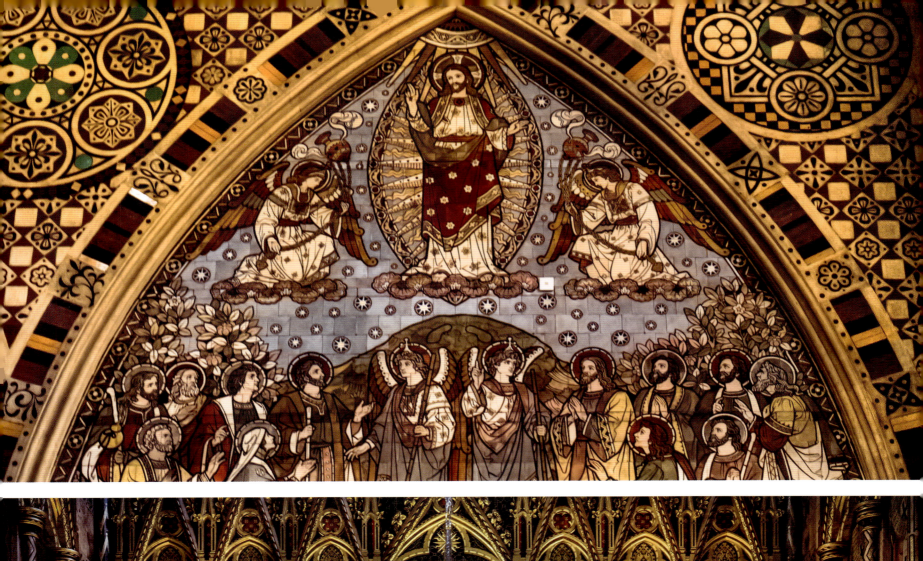

ALL SAINTS 163

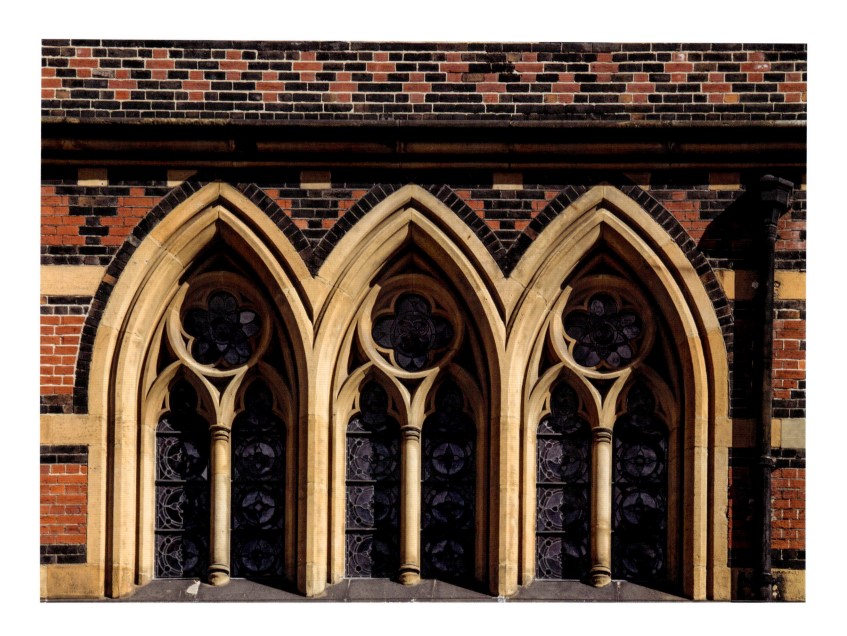

OPPOSITE: ABOVE This glorious tiled artwork on the north wall of the tower depicts the Ascension and was also a dedication to the much-revered churchwarden Henry Wood (d. 1891). BOTTOM The great silver pyx (Blessed Sacrament holder) hanging above the altar was another work by Comper.

ABOVE The nave's clerestory windows casting light down onto the sublime architecture and art of the church interior. Building a brick church in that era must have been difficult enough, but imagine having to lay every coloured brick with such inch-perfect symmetry.

St Augustine's

KILBURN PARK ROAD, NW6

St Augustine's has long been affectionately referred to as the 'cathedral of North London' and its architectural grandeur, impressive sculpture and sumptuous artwork certainly combine to make that title a worthy accolade. This magnificent Grade I-listed church was founded in 1870 by the Reverend Richard Carr Kirkpatrick, an Irish-born curate of another church in the district who had resigned his post three years earlier following the appointment of a new vicar whose attitudes and beliefs fell way below his own standards. Kilburn was housing many Irish immigrants and there were fears that total Catholicism would soon become dominant. With the support of other wealthy parishioners who shared his own fervent belief in the Anglo-Catholic movement, Kirkpatrick spent the next three years going through the process of gaining permission to establish a new parish from the Bishop of London, finding a suitable site and, most importantly, choosing an architect who would fulfil their hopes and dreams. The foundation stone was laid in 1871 and the church consecrated a decade later.

After much research, the Reverend Kirkpatrick had finally opted for John Loughborough Pearson (1817–97), one of the leading Victorian architects successfully replicating the Medieval Gothic style. The exterior has a spectacular west front with a large rose window framed by tall, narrow turrets, an abundance of narrow lancet windows and a steeple soaring up to 77.4m (254ft) high. The clean lines of the red brick and stone exterior were made possible by the most notable and structurally important feature: internal buttressing thought to have been inspired by the thirteenth-century cathedral of Albi in the Languedoc region of southern France. Being able to incorporate that internal support resulted in the absence of great blocks of stone blighting the exterior's visual harmony

The interior is a truly impressive sight, having been roofed throughout with Pearson's trademark ribbed vaulting, and has double aisles around the nave due to the internal buttressing. A first-floor gallery extending around three sides of the church provides viewpoints from which to appreciate the sheer size, architectural detail and the countless sculpted figures adorning the rood screen and chancel. In the spaces above the nave arches, there are also a series of colourful painted portrayals of Bible stories featuring Jesus. The rood screen is dominated by the central crucifix flanked on either side by key figures including Joseph of Arithamea, in whose sepulchre Christ was buried. Further representations of the Passion are sculpted on the screen panels, each portrayed in meticulously carved detail. The main east window comprises six lights in two tiers, several of which portray the life and work of the church's patron saint, the first Archbishop of Canterbury. The windows and much of the painted art throughout the church were executed by the firm of Clayton & Bell, one of the most prolific and artistically perfect studios of the Victorian era.

The church's north transept chapel is dedicated to Our Lady and is decorated with atmospheric frescoes depicting the infancy of Jesus. In complete artistic contrast, St Michael's Chapel in the south transept is just solid gold interspaced

---

The majestic red brick and pale stone exterior of St Augustine's was a stroke of genius by the commissioned architect, John Loughborough Pearson (1817–97). It perfectly reflected the aesthetic aspirations of the Oxford Anglo-Catholic Movement and was rightly awarded Grade I-listed status.

166 GREAT CHURCHES OF LONDON

with richly coloured artwork. All those elements are now substantially more vibrant than they might have appeared, as the chapel was restored just fifty years ago in 1973. The altar comprises three panels featuring angels at the Crucifixion in the centre; on the left they are ministering to Him at the Temptation and on the right they are with Jesus in Gethsemane. This chapel extends well back into the transept as there are several atmospheric murals all leading into that golden heart of St Michael's.

Although every element of this church is captivatingly beautiful, the real focal point of St Augustine's is the chancel, and as one passes through the rood screen, the predominantly brick interior of the nave is transformed into a graphic gallery of stone. None of the sculptures around the chancel screens are simply random, and the story of the Passion that began on the rood flows through into the chancel, past the organ and onto the reredos behind the high altar. The south wall of the transept contains figures of past archbishops of Canterbury and then thirteen saints, all portrayed in complex carvings. The chancel's marble floor is a truly magnificent piece of work that might have been inspired by Pearson's trips to Italy in the 1870s, but it could also be said that the Kilburn floor is not that dissimilar to the Cosmati Pavement in Westminster Abbey.

ABOVE St Michael's Chapel and part of the south transept merge into one glorious portfolio of gold, and its artwork is truly captivating. The reredos and figures in the apse depict St John's vision of Heaven in the Book of Revelations. Angels bearing musical instruments are everywhere.

OPPOSITE: TOP LEFT The Virgin Mary and Jesus on a banner used for processions at High Mass. TOP RIGHT The chancel's beautiful marble floor. BOTTOM Pictorial portrayals around the entire nave depicting the miracles of Jesus. OVERLEAF The absolutely beautiful chancel of St Augustine's is truly a major work of religious art.

Church of the Immaculate Conception

FARM STREET, W1

Farm Street lies towards the eastern side of Mayfair and close to both Grosvenor Square and Hyde Park. Its street name dates back to a time when Hay Hill Farm extended over a wide area in this locality, which went on to be transformed during the early decades of the eighteenth century. The principal landowners, Sir Richard Grosvenor and the Earl of Scarborough, began the development process and the aristocracy started moving westwards away from the cramped and outdated houses of the City and surrounding areas. It was around that time that the Jesuits were seeking a suitable site to establish their principal church, and it was in Farm Street that they managed to acquire a small parcel of land on which to build the Immaculate Conception. Yes, it may have been a cramped site and the church not able to be absolutely built in the customary east-west format, but those shortcomings were deemed less important than its location in the new 'heart of London'.

The Jesuit Order (also the Society of Jesus) was established in 1534 as a Catholic missionary order of priests and brothers by St Ignatius of Loyola (1491–1556) and formally approved by Pope Paul III in 1540. The current head of the Catholic Church, Pope Francis, is the first Jesuit Pope to have ever been elected. Fully professed Jesuits take the three customary vows of poverty, chastity and obedience, but also a fourth one that gives obedience to the Pope and to accept whatever worldwide mission they are requested to undertake. Catholicism had been a difficult and life-threatening road to tread since Henry VIII's 1534 Act of Supremacy created total severance of ties with Rome. It was really not until the Catholic Emancipation Act of 1829 that Britain officially accepted that its citizens were entitled to embrace Catholicism as their chosen religion.

Just over a decade later, in 1844, the architect J.J. Scoles (1798–1863) was commissioned to design and build the Farm Street church. In 1822 he had departed on a tour of Europe, the Middle East and North Africa for architectural and archaeological research, returning four years later to resume his career with a stash of sketchbooks and architectural drawings for reference and inspiration. However, when it came to designing the Immaculate Conception, his vision was firmly locked onto the Gothic style and he created a beautiful church based mainly on the fourteenth-century Decorated period but in a more flowing and exuberant style. The magnificent west front of the church was inspired by Beauvais Cathedral in France, and despite its ornate stonework and a complex rose window, the church does not visually impede on the architectural serenity of its surroundings.

The interior is beautifully structured with an eight-bay-long nave ending at the chancel. There is a chancel arch but as it is very tall and with no rood screen it makes the atmosphere of the church more inclusive. One significant alteration to the original layout resulted in the sanctuary floor, altar, reredos and nine-light east window being raised to ensure that those most important elements of the church became even more visible to the congregation. The high altar and reredos were

---

Immaculate Conception was created for the Jesuits who sought a site for this major church in a prominent part of London, and being in Mayfair certainly fulfilled those ideals. It was modelled on a French cathedral and its west front is a portfolio of elegant stonework.

CHURCH OF THE IMMACULATE CONCEPTION

actually designed by Augustus Pugin (1812–52), who was acknowledged as the pioneer of the Victorian Gothic Revival and is one of the best artists associated with church design during that exciting period.

Although the church was completed in 1849, just five years after the foundation stone was laid, work did not stop and there were almost constant amendments and additions as the years passed. One of the most significant periods was in the 1870s when a small parcel of land became available enabling the addition of a south aisle. This now comprises three substantial chapels and a porch leading onto Farm Street, and a north aisle was added at the end of the nineteenth century with more chapels being created. These are all impressive structures, the most imposing being the Chapel of St Ignatius Loyola, outside of which stands a black-clad marble statue that represents their habit or dress. In stark contrast, another chapel is dedicated to St Anthony of Padua, whose statue is carved from gleaming white Carrara marble. The octagonal Calvary Chapel located at the church's west end was actually transformed into a baptistery in 1966 when the church was finally awarded parish status and thereby able to conduct weddings and baptisms.

OPPOSITE The interior of Immaculate Conception is an impressive portfolio of architecture, artwork, glass and colour. The set of clerestory windows is not overly laden with stained glass, thereby enabling plenty of light to flood into the nave and side chapels lining the north and south aisles.

ABOVE The side chapels were added after the main church was built and their artistic grandeur renders some of them to be almost churches in their own right, but despite that, there are still beautiful individual pieces of sculpture such as this rendering of the Virgin and Child.

St Mary Magdalene

PADDINGTON, W2

St Mary Magdalene is readily accessible from central London via the Bakerloo Line up to Warwick Avenue station. From there it is just a gentle stroll to the banks of the Grand Union Canal. A left turn leads to the affluent area of Little Venice, but a right turn gives access to a pedestrian bridge that crosses the canal and, from there, the view towards St Mary Magdalene is most impressive. Trees rise up between the church and the canal's north bank, a footpath runs parallel with the waterway and there are also children's play areas and small public patches of greenery in the vicinity. The tall pointed spire of St Mary's soars high above its surroundings and has done so ever since its completion in 1872. The parish of St Mary Magdalene was created in 1865 as a 'church plant' from All Saints, Margaret Street, by its curate Father Richard Temple West (1827–93), who was appointed vicar of St Mary's in that same year, a post retained until his death. He was a highly respected and prominent member of the Anglo-Catholic High Church movement flourishing around that period. It must have been a monumental task of faith, love and perseverance to get that new church filled by the population of what was then one of London's most densely packed slum districts. Black and white archive photographs of the church from the early twentieth century reveal what a challenging task the church's design and construction must have been.

There might have been the assumption that such impoverished communities needed little more than a basic church, but the flourishing Anglo-Catholic movement thought exactly the opposite. Their reintroduction of dramatic Gothic architectural styles served as an almost theatrical background for services full of colour, music and ritual that would temporarily transport people away from their poverty-stricken lives of misery. Of course, that brief opening of the door of hope created such a welcoming feeling that those who enjoyed it returned again and again to become enthusiastic members of that family of Faith.

The architect commissioned with that task was the acclaimed George Edmund Street (1824–81), who was also a member of the Margaret Street congregation. The creation of a Gothic Revival church in this location must have seemed a daunting assignment but Street managed to overcome the challenges. His working life at that particular time must have been quite traumatic, because not only was he having to design and build a large church on a small and uneven site, he was also creating the Royal Courts of Justice on the Strand. Due to its close proximity to the canal banks, the site sloped steeply from north to south but also had levelling issues elsewhere, and was so hemmed in by housing that the church's west end was virtually butting right up to the final house of a long terrace. So tight was the available space that there was room for an aisle only on the south side, where the steeple is also squeezed in next to the small transept.

The focal point of every church is the chancel, and the area immediately behind the altar is called the apse. In many churches it was simply a straight line of wall and windows at

---

The Chapel of the Holy Sepulchre in the undercroft was the first London commission of Sir John Ninian Comper (1864–1960) and dedicated to Father Richard Temple West, the church's first vicar. This photograph was taken during restoration, hence the few unfinished painted panels.

176 Great Churches of London

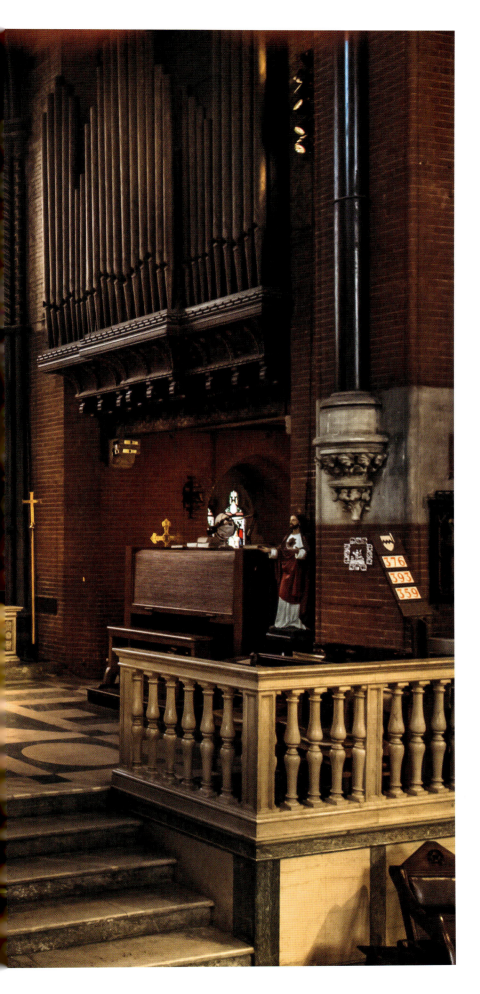

the east end, but St Mary Magdalene was furnished with a semi-circular version more commonly associated with French and other European churches. The design of this one is not only visually dramatic, but also moving in the way that the elaborately decorated walls and story-telling stained glass windows curve round to respectfully and lovingly embrace the altar. A couple of decades later the upper echelons of the Anglo-Catholic movement decided that Baroque was the only architectural style to embrace, and so changes were made where possible; in the case of St Mary's, the chancel floor level was raised and extended further towards the nave, where it was enclosed in a beautiful marble balustrade.

During the 1960s, most of the local housing was demolished in a massive post-war slum clearance and the congregation consequently declined. The condition of the church was also heading the same way and it was not until the early twenty-first century that funding was accessed to not only halt the decay but also undertake a massive cleaning and conservation programme that has transformed so much of the outstanding artwork that was fading into obscurity. Affectionately called St Mary Mag's by its parishioners, Street's architectural gem looks well set for an extremely protracted journey into future decades.

The chancel is considered one of Street's finest, and its walls are covered in alabaster panels and mosaics from the Salviati works of the Venetian island of Murano, famed for its glasswork. Henry Holiday was responsible for the glass in both the chancel and other windows.

OPPOSITE: TOP The chancel windows by Henry Holiday depict scenes from the life of Christ. BOTTOM LEFT The ceiling panels in both the chancel and nave were painted by Daniel Bell and are now all fully visible after recent restoration. BOTTOM RIGHT The undercroft chapel's altar.

ABOVE St Mary Magdalene is a large church with beautiful statues of both the Virgin Mary and Mary Magdalene. In this one, the right hand of Jesus is crafted in the same gesture adopted by priests when offering blessings to the congregation in the shape of a cross.

180 Great Churches of London

ABOVE AND OPPOSITE The colours and detail of the Holy Sepulcre Chapel are really quite mesmerizing, and the ceiling is aglow with gilded stars and richly painted images of angels. One can only imagine what it must have looked like under candlelight. At the opposite end of the chapel and facing back towards the altar stands the remarkable organ case featuring decorative patterns that frame a diptych of Mary Magdalene and Jesus in the garden on the morning of his Resurrection. When Mary recognizes Jesus he responds with the famous phrase *noli me tangere* ('touch me not').

London Oratory

BROMPTON ROAD, SW7

The London Oratory is usually, but incorrectly, called the Brompton Oratory, probably due to a combination of its web address bearing that name and its location on Brompton Road's junction with Cromwell Road. The latter's final stage runs past the Natural History and Victoria and Albert Museums, and that grouping of very English buildings gives way to a genuine slice of Italian church architecture. The church actually has two very full formal titles: the Congregation of the Oratory of Saint Philip Neri and the Church of the Immaculate Heart of Mary. The Italian religious group called the Congregation of the Oratory was founded in Rome by St Philip Neri (1515–95) as part of the renewal of the Catholic Church after the Reformation.

Two English Catholic priests, who both sought deeper answers to their own beliefs, travelled to Rome and became involved in the Oratory group. Father John Henry Newman (1801–90) had converted to Catholicism in 1845 and became a sincere supporter of the English Oxford Movement that favoured the way Catholics designed their churches and the glorious manner in which they conducted Mass. His companion and Catholic convert was Frederick William Faber (1814–63), and upon their return to England Newman decided to settle in Birmingham, and thus it was Faber who set up the London Oratory in 1854. Although Knightsbridge and South Kensington are very much part of today's central London, Father Faber then lauded the wonderful views of Kensington Gardens. Initially, the Oratory used a temporary church in 1854 but it was not until 1880–84 that the great Italianate church was built according to designs of the chosen architect Herbert Gribble (1847–94). Even then, the west front and dome were still missing and they took another decade to make the masterpiece complete and just as we see it today. In outlining his architectural plans for the Oratory, Gribble stated that if people were not able to travel all the way to Italy, Brompton could be a viable option, given the patronage of the church. The dome is actually taller than originally planned but as a result it does make the church significantly more of a landmark.

The basic fabric of the building may have been completed but its complex array of chapels, statues and memorials erected along the aisles flanking either side of the very wide three-bay nave were gradually added piece by piece. Some of those elements were created by local artists and craftsmen but some notable pieces were imported from Europe. One of the most significant is the Lady Altar that actually came from a Dominican church in Brescia, northern Italy, that was being demolished and its contents offered up for sale. The statue of the Virgin, also known as Our Lady of Victories, was not part of that purchase as it belonged to the original London church used prior to the Oratory's construction. Another major acquisition was the twelve seventeenth-century marble statues of the Apostles that came from Siena Cathedral. Herbert Gribble himself designed a number of the most important altars, some of which are so architecturally elaborate that

This famous Roman Catholic church was established in London for the Congregation of the Oratory of St Philip Neri towards the latter stages of the nineteenth century. To the left of the dramatic main entrance sits a beautiful memorial statue to its founder, John Henry Newman.

184 Great Churches of London

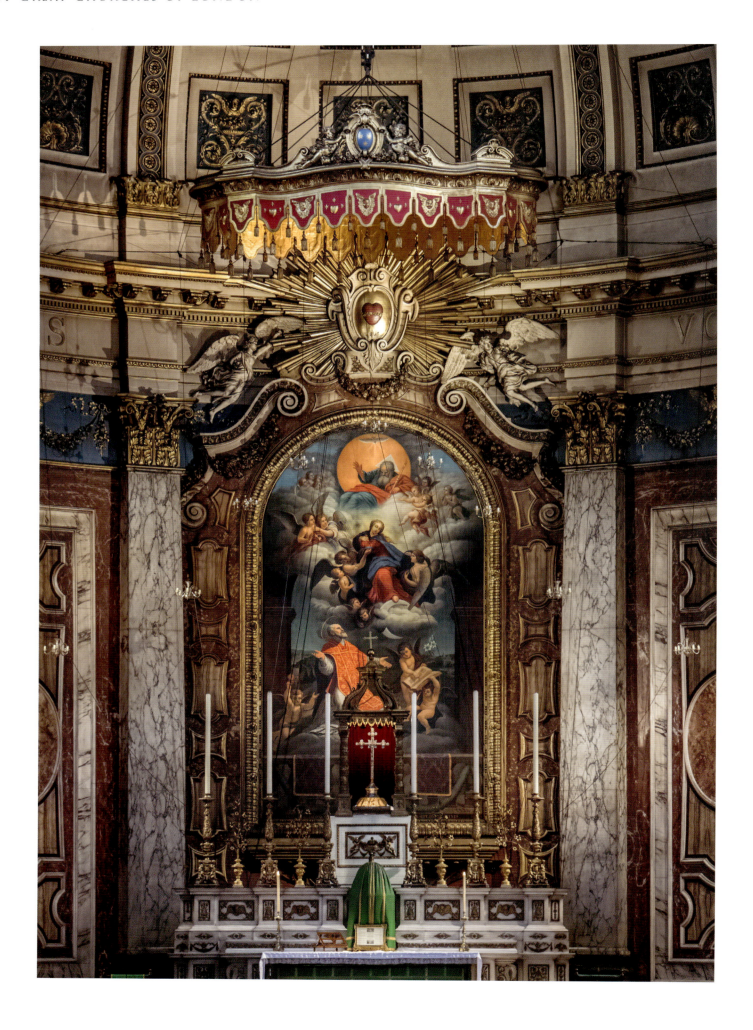

one feels that they should not be obscured by the arches and pillars of the nave. However, there is the important element of personal privacy that is sustained where possible for those seeking a period of quiet contemplation.

One of the more intriguing altars tucked away in the south-east corner of the nave and adjacent to the high altar is St Wilfred's Chapel. This was originally the high altar in a Belgian monastic church, which was transferred in 1811 to the Basilica of St Servatius in Maastricht (Netherlands) and finally made it across the sea to London. That entire chapel was donated by a private person as a memorial to the Oratory's first Provost, Father Faber, whose body now lies under the floor in front of the main altar. Another altar occupying that chapel is dedicated to the English Martyrs and set above is the only known religious painting by Rex Whistler. It is in the form of triptych and portrays saints Thomas More and John Fisher on either side with a quite grim execution scene taking place at Tyburn in the centre.

Religious art, furniture and sculpture are obviously viewable during the daily opening hours but the lighting is often quite minimal. However, if one attends a Mass or other service featuring one of the Oratory's three brilliant choirs and musicians, it would be a truly moving and memorable event to savour.

OPPOSITE The impressive high altar stands in the very deep sanctuary and is perfectly structured for the solemn celebration of Mass. It managed to escape the changes imposed by Vatican II in the 1960s that required altars to be turned round to face the congregation.

ABOVE The pair of elegant seven-branched candlesticks standing on marble plinths in the sanctuary were modelled on those originally set in the Temple of Jerusalem. OVERLEAF A view down the Oratory's nave past the pulpit and on into the beautifully formed sanctuary.

St Mary's

BOURNE STREET, SW1

St Mary's was built in 1874 and originally intended as a chapel of ease to St Paul's, Knightsbridge, and a place of worship for the increasingly large servant population associated with the neighbouring wealthy districts. The expansion of London during the Victorian era demanded a significant acceleration of church building, as declining to attend church in those days was not really an option, and so significantly more had to be built to match the housing development. The original version of St Mary's was a quite basic red brick structure built directly over the London Underground's District Line, whose trains still create a soft rumble coming up through the floor. To sustain the economic restrictions, low windowless aisles were created and the roof was made of plain slate topped by a bellcote housing a solitary bell. When the church was initially constructed, its entrance was on the adjacent Graham Terrace rather than Bourne Street, and that street actually only received its name in 1938. The architect for the original church was Robert Jewell Withers (1824–94), whose church comprised a high, broad nave separated from the narrow aisles by five bay arcades set on cylindrical stone piers, with carved capitals that continued round the semi-circular apse and blind arches on brick piers. Despite having been created for significantly less than many other fairly basic churches, its design, layout and decor was nevertheless praised by the *Church Times* writer who had attended the dedication on 4 July 1874 and cited St Mary's as being 'an excellent specimen of an inexpensive church'. It was subsequently designated a parish church in 1909 and from that significant moment of status elevation, St Mary's ecclesiastical and social care was increasingly welcomed by its new parishioners.

Having become a parish in its own right, its first vicar, Father Cyril Howell, commissioned the church architect Sidney Gambier-Parry (1859–1948) to replace the reredos. Rising up behind the altar, a reredos is a visually captivating element for the congregation that always plays a significant role in the ceremonial presentation of the Mass and, given St Mary's newly elevated status, Father Howell knew what needed to be achieved. Consequently, an Elizabethan-style arch made from dark wood decorated with elaborate strapwork and topped by a dramatic sunburst was created to generate renewed enthusiasm and respect from the congregation. Father Howell's successor continued escalating the standing of the sanctuary, and the next commissioned craftsman was Martin Travers (1886–1948), who went on to become one of the most influential stained glass artists of the twentieth century. He created a sarcophagus-like altar of gilded wood on raised steps with a domed and gilded tabernacle flanked on either side by six beautiful Baroque-style candlesticks (now replaced by close replicas).

St Mary's artistic and architectural progress continued and was substantially amended in the 1920s by the much respected and prolific church architect H.S. Goodhart-Rendel CBE (1887–1959). He completely changed its main point of access

---

The visual drama of the high altar and reredos has been accentuated by being set in a curved apse rather than against a straight wall. The partially coloured windows are effective in preventing glare without diminishing the illumination in the manner of full stained glass panels.

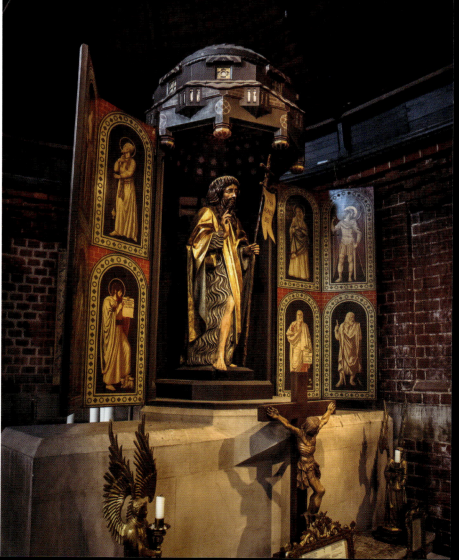

by demolishing a house adjacent to the Pineapple public house that stood on the corner of Bourne Street and Graham Terrace and created a polygonal porch to be St Mary's new entrance. It is so well set back along a narrow passageway that it is actually quite easy to walk right past before realizing one's mistake. Goodhart-Rendel also undertook several other important projects relating to the church's interior, to such an extent that it started to establish quite a reputation and moved higher up the congregational ladder than had originally been intended or expected. Although those internal works that included a new side chapel were important in the church's architectural and artistic progression, another structural event made huge differences for both clergy and parishioners.

The Pineapple pub was acquired by the church, and in 1922 went from pub to presbytery following a significant remodelling by Goodhart-Rendel. Due to its previous role, the building's layout was a complex design issue but the highly talented architect did such a masterful transformation that it was designated a Grade II-listed building. The first floor library and dining rooms are atmospheric and still with the same layouts and furnishings. The year 2024 marks St Mary's 150th anniversary and the Pineapple Project is at the heart of its continued work in providing both pastoral and religious care to those in the community. The church has been upgraded over the years and with a great musical tradition remains a much-revered church in the Anglo-Catholic movement.

OPPOSITE: TOP LEFT AND RIGHT Two of the many statues adorning the walls of St Mary's. BOTTOM LEFT Our Lady of Peace created by Martin Travers, who also did much other significant work in St Mary's. BOTTOM RIGHT The altar and tabernacle of St John the Baptist were designed by Goodhart-Rendel and the statue was by Harold Gibbons.

ABOVE A view from Graham Terrace of the simple 'budget' church, constructed from machine-made red bricks, and its simple bellcote and spire rising above a plain slated roof. The church exterior may be simple but inside is a different matter.

192 GREAT CHURCHES OF LONDON

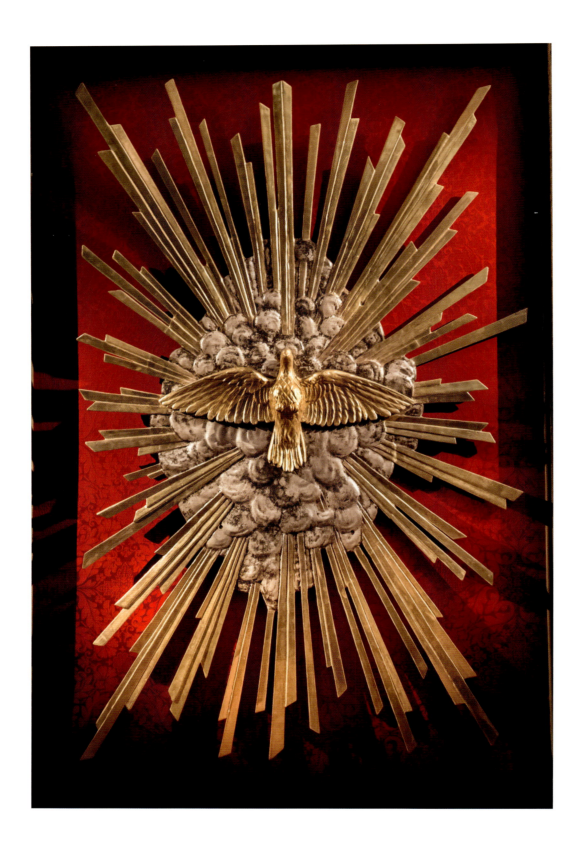

ABOVE The symbolic dove has many relationships with the Church. One of its most significant appearances was at the baptism of Jesus Christ, and earlier in the Noah's Ark saga when bringing back the olive branch that has forever made it the symbol of peace and hope.

OPPOSITE The reredos to the altar of the Seven Sorrows of Our Lady was painted by Colin Gill (1892–1940) and depicts six of the seven sorrows in two lines, with the final panel below the Deposition of Christ from the Cross.

St Cuthbert's

PHILBEACH GARDENS, SW5

When the Victorian builders were constructing houses around the almost perfect semi-circle of Philbeach Gardens in Earl's Court during the 1870s, they had to punctuate that symmetry with a space to accommodate the church and associated buildings of St Cuthbert's. It was constructed between 1884–7, rising dramatically among the elegant Victorian terraced houses, although a clear frontal view is now somewhat obscured by one of the trees that started out as decorative saplings many decades ago. However, by just walking for a couple of hundred yards along the pavement flanking the main A4 dual carriageway, a completely different façade is proffered.

This elevated section gives a clear view of the church and instead of being built with a tower, a tall, slender flèche soars high above the dark slate roof. The original roof was seriously damaged during the Second World War and rebuilt with copper sheeting, a choice that saw the almost total demise of St Cuthbert's as major leaks occurred and rainwater cascaded down into sections of the church. Because there were so many other parish churches in the Earl's Court district, it was as recently as 1986 that the Archdeacon of Middlesex suggested that St Cuthbert's should close. Fortunately, a major rescue campaign was elevated to the Bishop of London in the House of Lords and subsequent grants from English Heritage and the Heritage Lottery Fund succeeded in the funding of a new Westmorland slate roof with lead guttering. Had that rescue attempt failed, London would have lost a fine portfolio from the Arts & Crafts movement.

St Cuthbert's was named after the seventh-century Saxon monk associated with the significant spread of Christianity from the monastery established on Lindisfarne (Holy Island) set just off the north Northumbrian coast. The church is fortunate to be in the possession of four relics of its patron saint, two of which were small pieces of the untarnished garment in which he was interred, and the others fragments of his original wood coffin. All four were lawfully obtained during two openings of St Cuthbert's tomb in Durham Cathedral, and the reliquary in which they are preserved is placed on the high altar on St Cuthbert's feast days in March and September. That direct link with Lindisfarne had initially been established when a specially excavated piece of rock was brought to London and laid as the church's foundation stone. The chosen architect was Hugh Roumieu Gough (1843–1904), who designed a high nave and continuous chancel in a rich Decorated period Gothic style. To enter St Cuthbert's for the first time is a truly awesome experience due to the dark richness of its interior. The nave pillars are made from solid marble in a variety of colours and the walls panelled in similar material and then hung with large Stations of the Cross. The clerestory windows cast light down on to the dramatic rood beam and its large carved figures (pages 156–7). The first vicar was Father Henry Westall, who served non-stop until his death in 1924, and it was his drive, enthusiasm and total commitment to

---

St Cuthbert's was consecrated in 1887 and has twin façades of differing colours and materials. This distant view of its red brick body with a slender flèche is a fascinating contrast to its main façade on Philbeach Gardens that veers firmly back towards the Early Gothic period.

the Anglo-Catholic faith that established St Cuthbert's as a serious High Church.

A lot of the interior decor was created by a major community effort over many years in which members of the congregation were organized into a variety of Arts and Crafts Guilds. They all progressed under professional direction and played a significant role in getting the church lavishly embellished. One particularly noteworthy contributor was W. Bainbridge Reynolds, who specialized in handmade metalwork and was responsible for creating many of the church's eye-catching works of art. His major triumph was the lectern created from wrought iron and copper supporting a complex platform to which leather supports for the books are lashed by leather thongs and two candleholders swing out on either side. He also executed metal screens at the end of the nave aisles, beautifully engraved communion rails and several large candlesticks.

However, even Mr Reynolds' portfolio was overshadowed by the single work of Father Ernest Geldart, who designed the unpainted wood reredos that rises to the full height of the east end and was entitled 'The Worship of the Incarnate Son of God with Incense and Lights'. There are many scenes from the Bible, the Evangelists, many saints plus countless others all immaculately carved. The reredos was eventually installed in 1914 just prior to the start of the First World War and its presence created a harmonious sense of completion throughout the church at a most appropriate time.

OPPOSITE The beautifully decorated altar is a true reflection of the church's High Catholic status but even that is somewhat overwhelmed by the reredos soaring up to the full height of the east end. It was installed in 1914 and is just the most amazing portfolio of carved art.

ABOVE When the feast day of St Cuthbert is celebrated on 20 March, the already superb furnishings and altar decorations are increased again, and this handmade altar cloth really is an incredibly executed piece of art that must have taken ages to create with such finesse.

198 Great Churches of London

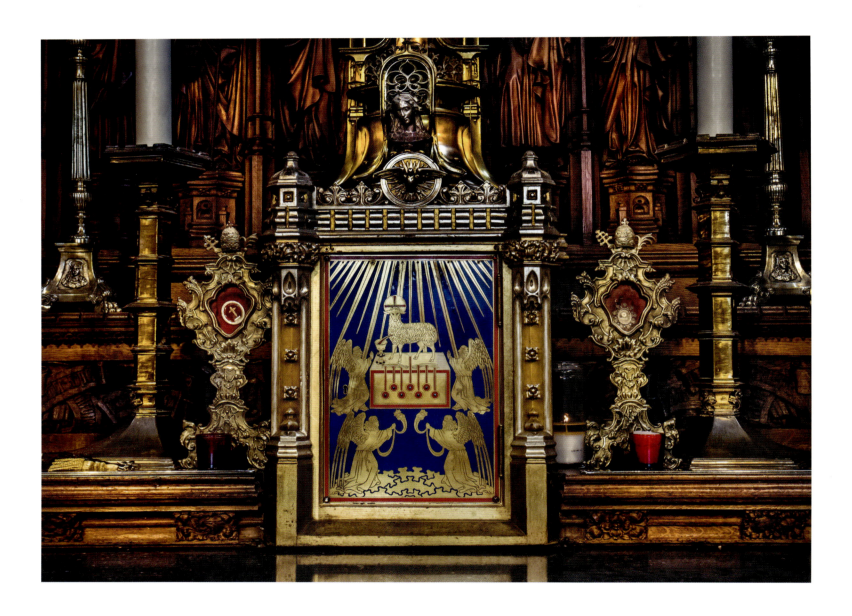

ABOVE The high altar's strikingly beautiful tabernacle was designed and made by William Bainbridge Reynolds just two years before his death in 1935. He was an extraordinary creative metalwork artist who made many other significant contributions to the Arts & Crafts portfolio of St Cuthbert's.

OPPOSITE The Lady Chapel is another amazing portfolio of metalwork, painted art, glass and sculpture. The ceiling bears a painted depiction of the Virgin and Child flanked by angels, and there is also a beautiful flock of cherub heads designed by the Italian sculptor Andrea Lucchesi.

Union Chapel

COMPTON TERRACE, ISLINGTON N1

The Union Chapel is located in the midst of an elegant row of Georgian terraced houses that were erected between 1805 and 1831 as upmarket townhouses for professionals working in the City. They were set back from the noisy road of Upper Street that leads up to Islington, and the strip of land between the main road and houses was allowed to be transformed into a beautiful garden area for residents. That main road is actually the A1 and although busy with traffic now, it was probably even more chaotic back in the early nineteenth century as it was the main route into London from Scotland, the Midlands and north of England, resulting in huge numbers of cattle being driven down to the meat markets each week.

The initial chapel was built towards the northern end of the terrace in 1806 following the association of groups of men from differing approaches to Christian worship who had collectively decided that their own particular churches were not fulfilling their spiritual needs. They were mainly comprised of Episcopalians and Nonconformists who felt that more evangelical worship was the direction in which they needed to direct their Christian faith. The new place of worship they constructed was called the Union Chapel to clearly indicate that despite their individual varieties of religious belief, they were actually all united.

During those early days they ran different kinds of services in the morning and evening to ensure that every member was able to continue along their own particular route of Christian worship. Their intention was to ensure that the Union Chapel was regarded as a 'Friend for All', and that ethos continues to the present day. From 1844–92 the chapel was endowed with an outstanding minister, Henry Allon, who significantly elevated its status to the extent that several leading politicians became regular members of the congregation. As decades passed, the population of Islington and Highbury increased so rapidly that over two dozen Anglican and Nonconformist churches were built to cater for those numbers.

The Union Chapel was also becoming over-burdened by an ever-increasing congregation to such an extent that it was decided a new chapel was the only way to successfully maintain its important role in that expanding population. An architectural competition ensued and the winner was James Cubitt (1836–1914), an architect who specialized in Nonconformist places of worship. His church- and chapel-building philosophy was clearly laid out in a published book entitled *Church Design for Congregations*, which lampooned the traditional nave and aisle design of churches. His view was that in church naves supported by large pillars, a significant proportion of the congregation would have little or no view.

With the exception of the tower that was added a few years later, the work was undertaken between 1876–7 and the Union Chapel is now accredited with the status of a Grade I-listed building. Cubitt had maintained his architectural philosophy and created a massive, slightly irregular-shaped octagon set within a rectangle and crowned with a huge top-

---

The Union Chapel was built by architect James Cubitt, who specialized in building Nonconformist Christian churches and chapels. The tower and façade are in Gothic style and the elegant arches and windows feature more prominently, having been created from contrasting pale stone.

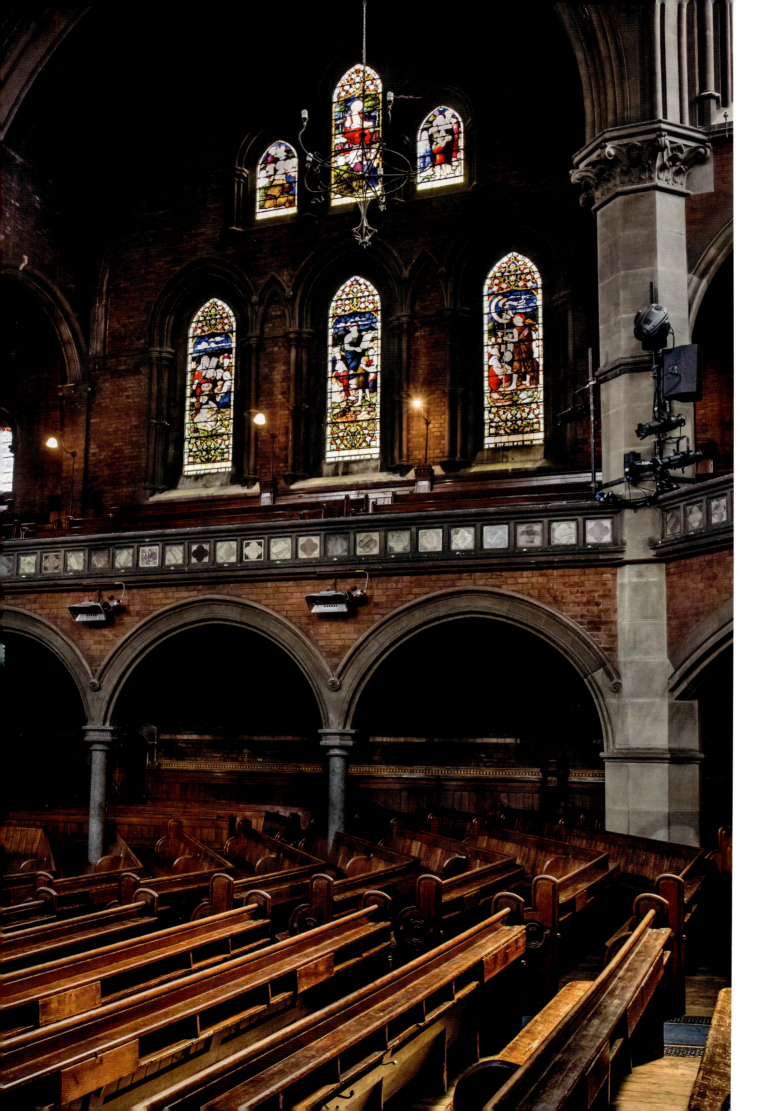

Union Chapel 203

lit dome. It was designed to seat 1,700 and also had a large Sunday school hall at the rear to accommodate almost 1,000 children. The heating for such a voluminous room was a serious undertaking and successfully achieved by pumping hot water from a boiler in the cellar up through a network of large-diameter pipes with regular grilles along the main gangways.

What the late-nineteenth-century chapel did not have were the speakers and spotlights now attached to every pillar around the outer arches of the octagon because the Union Chapel has become one of London's most celebrated concert venues. However, although there will always be access to a variety of music from every imaginable genre, the chapel's musical 'star' has been there for quite some time, though nobody has ever been able to see it. The Grade I-listed organ is deliberately invisible, with the organist hidden behind the pulpit and its pipes secreted behind a screen so that the music floats elegantly upwards into the acoustically perfect dome.

The tall, elegant tower with its external clock set at right angles has been a distinctive part of the Islington landscape for almost 150 years and must be an especially welcome landmark to those making their way to Union Chapel seeking help from the Margins Project. Founded in 1995, the project is currently managing to help some 200 people a week who are homeless, facing homelessness or dealing with other major crises.

OPPOSITE The six lancet windows in the south wall are by Lavers and Westlake and show Christ plus scenes of preaching featuring Moses, Isaiah and John the Baptist.

ABOVE The symmetrically perfect rows of pews are well heated and all have perfect vision towards the pulpit, altar or the stage on which bands or solo artists are performing.

204 Great Churches of London

The eight-arched wood dome of the chapel is an impeccably designed and carved piece of work that harmonizes perfectly with the surrounding stone and brickwork.

UNION CHAPEL 205

A dramatically created stained glass angel with the most phenomenal set of red feathered wings and sword stands guard over the east gallery of the chapel.

St Cyprian's

GLENTWORTH STREET, NW1

The parish of St Cyprian was established in Marylebone by Father Charles Gutch in 1866. It was at a time when London's rapidly expanding population was making it increasingly difficult for churches to provide parochial care to those areas where poverty was rife. Despite having to overcome problems generated by the wealthy local landowner, Father Gutch eventually managed to establish a Mission Church created from two small houses and a hayloft close by the western corner of Regent's Park. Upon his death thirty years later, the diminutive church was still struggling to accommodate its parishioners, but the combined efforts of both a new parish priest and the Bishop of London finally managed to successfully negotiate a deal for a plot of land with the Portland Estate on what is now Glentworth Street. St Cyprian's lies at the end of that road, seamlessly butted onto the end of a long line of elegant seven-storey Victorian mansion blocks.

The chosen architect was Sir John Ninian Comper (1864–1960) who, at the time of his commission, was vociferously lauding the English Gothic Perpendicular as being the most appropriate style for the Anglo-Catholic Gothic Revival. The Dedication service was held on 30 June 1903, albeit in a church interior which at that stage was little more than a shell. All the distinctive architectural and artistic features that combine to make St Cyprian's a building of such impressive style were added over the next few decades. The church has no tower or steeple and the only external visual clue to its identity is the line of tall windows topped by a matching set of smaller clerestory glass above. However, the contrast between exterior and interior could not be more breathtakingly dramatic, and as one enters the nave there is not a hint of drab brick or stonework in sight. Comper's interpretation of the Perpendicular style was simply predominantly white and gold interspersed with exquisitely executed artworks.

The high arches and aisles of the nave are beautifully lit by the combination of Perpendicular-style windows and the clerestory, a lightness accentuated by the absence of dark pews that fill many churches. That absence of heavy seating does reveal a tarnished area of the south aisle floor caused by incendiary bombs that fell on the roof and then down into the church during a 1940 air raid. Fortunately, the fire brigade were able to save the roof and volunteers extinguished the fire below, and that scarred part of the church has been left as a memorial. So many London churches were damaged and successfully renovated but one senses that the artistic delicacy of St Cyprian's might have been difficult to recreate, even though Comper's son, Sebastian, assumed responsibility for the art and architecture of the church.

Although St Cyprian's is enriched with individual pieces of art, the painted and gilded rood screen completed in 1924 has to be the most visually mesmerizing. There are thirty-two painted figures in its lower panels, with the ones on either side of the Lady Chapel entrance all being portraits of women. The traditional rood figures with Christ Crucified at the centre are

---

Although built in the early twentieth century, St Cyprian's could easily be mistaken for a church built centuries earlier, and that was absolutely the objective of its creator, Sir Ninian Comper, who sought to take the design of his churches back to the Gothic era.

also richly painted and gilded. High above the screen is the *Majestas*, a painting that forms the roof break between nave and chancel. It was restored in 1997, making the complex detail so much more visible from ground level. Our Lord in Glory is flanked by the twelve Apostles and surrounded by rays of light, His feet rest on a globe and in the corners are trumpet-blowing angels.

The glorious sanctuary housing the high altar is flanked by the Holy Name Chapel whose unusual metal and wood altar screen of black and gold was created in 1938.

The adjacent sanctuary houses the remarkably large high altar made from one very thick stone slab 4.1m (13ft 6in) long. It is flanked by side curtains secured to four posts surmounted by candle-bearing angels. The front and rear panels of the high altar are directly linked in a complex narrative starting with Adam and Eve and leading up to the Crucifixion at Golgotha.

On the other side of the high altar, the Lady Chapel stands on the site of the old Mission Church House occupied by the founder of St Cyprian's during his latter years. A most moving memorial brass to Father Gutch is set into the floor of the chapel, and were it not for his intense devotion and resolution, there might never have been a St Cyprian's.

OPPOSITE Although there is much art and architecture to admire, the most captivating is the gilded rood screen completed in 1924. It starts two bays from the east end and stretches across the nave and aisles and has thirty-two painted figures in its lower panels.

ABOVE Set high above the altar is a large tester, or sounding board, made from wood and elaborately painted in oils. Around the figure of Christ are several written pieces in Greek, the open book bearing the words, 'I am the Light of the World'.

210 Great Churches of London

The altar of St Cyprian's has side curtains supported by four riddel posts topped with candle-bearing gold angels. The table itself was made from one very thick piece of stone and is now shrouded in the front and rear dossals that combine to tell one story.

ST CYPRIAN'S 211

The frontal of the altar is the most exquisitely embroidered piece of fabric whose focal point is the Garden of Eden. The Tree of Knowledge then winds up to the fossal at the altar's rear where it becomes transformed into the Tree of Life on which Jesus was crucified.

St Jude's-on-the-Hill

Hampstead Garden Suburb, NW11

As London expanded outwards from its medieval City walls, most of those newly established communities would have been designated suburbs, as that definition simply means 'an outlying district of a city'. Hampstead Garden Suburb is not only unique in having that word included in its title, but also in the manner in which it was created. In the first decade of the twentieth century, this fashionable new suburb was established by Henrietta Barnett (1851–1936) and her husband, Canon Samuel Barnett (1844–1913), who was the vicar of St Jude's in Whitechapel. Both had worked tirelessly in that desperately deprived area of east London and, after several years, decided to buy a house in Hampstead where they could retreat for a couple of nights. In 1896 Henrietta happened to meet an American entrepreneur who mentioned that he was planning to extend the Underground further north up to what is now Golders Green station. She immediately had a vision of rows and rows of houses pinched together as tightly as the Whitechapel slums and spreading up onto the slopes of Hampstead Heath. She mounted a massive campaign to prevent such a thing happening and in two phases managed to purchase over 300 acres of land that Eton College had received from Henry VIII in an earlier compensation deal.

Henrietta's ambition was to create a community where both rich and poor could live side by side, and that ethos was the inspiration behind the establishment of Hampstead Garden Suburb. She formed a prominent team that included Lord Crewe, a high-ranking member of the House of Lords, and it was with him one day that she trudged over the Heath's rough terrain to its highest point. It was on the summit that she declared it ought to be there that the 'houses of learning and worship' should be established. In 1905 Henrietta set out her scheme, followed by massive fund-raising events, and on 2 May 1907 she ceremoniously turned a spadeful of soil on a site where the first cottages were to be built. Sir Edwin Lutyens (1869–1944) was one of Britain's finest architects, and although involved in the planning and design of the Suburb and its houses, his primary role was the creation of two places of worship: the Free Church and St Jude's still face each other across the verdant, tree-flanked Central Square lined with elegant houses. Building began in 1909 and was finally completed in 1935.

The exterior of St Jude's is a visually compelling combination of architectural styles from different eras with the 54m (177ft) glistening white Gothic steeple creating a dramatic impression. The steeple is set upon a tower modelled on the Byzantine era with tiered open brick arches, and the very steeply pitched nave roof dips almost to the ground. Everything about St Jude's exterior is visually captivating but some architectural critics have been significantly less enthused about the predominantly brick interior with painted art everywhere. However, in the published guide to St Jude's there is a reproduction of a painting portraying the chancel and altar prior to the artwork being added, and it is very disconcerting

---

The chancel and sanctuary with its green and white marble altar created by Sir Edwin Lutyens. The organ was originally in St Jude's, Whitechapel, where Canon Samuel Barnett was vicar from 1872–93. It was rededicated in 2002 after extensive renovation and the addition of a new console.

looking at the vast interior with high domes, roofs and walls comprised solely of white paint and red brick.

Most of the art is accredited to Walter P. Starmer (1877–1961), who spent more than a decade working on the walls, domes, arches and ceilings. Just about every single piece of his artistry was related to specific events and people in the Bible. The Lady Chapel was the first segment of the church completed and opened for worship in 2010 and, although it was there that Starmer began creating his portfolio, he did not actually begin until 1920 due to his involvement in the First World War. He was a volunteer with the Red Cross and YMCA and also one of the many artists who took their basic equipment to the trenches, and a significant collection of his works from that time are now lodged with the Imperial War Museum. One extremely moving brass plaque memorial related to the war is set on the north wall close by the west door: 'In Grateful memory of the Empire's horses (some 375,000) who fell in the Great War. Most obediently and most often painfully they died.'

There is much to savour in St Jude's and it is a church so renowned for its interior's visual and acoustic qualities, wide aisles and easy access that it is frequently used as a film location and a venue for orchestral recordings.

ABOVE One of the nave's central ceiling panels depicts Jesus steadying the storm on a ship with a caption from Isaiah 26:3 stating 'thou wilt keep him in perfect peace'. The paintings were replicated on either side to enable clear viewing from both sets of pews.

OPPOSITE: TOP LEFT The spire and tower of St Jude's. TOP RIGHT The nave's ceiling paintings. BOTTOM A panel in the Lady Chapel features a foundation stone by Eric Gill laid on 25 April 1910, now enclosed within a mural commemorating the dead of the First World War.

THIS STONE
WAS LAID BY
THE RIGHT HON.
EARL OF CREWE. K.G.
ON THE FEAST
OF S. MARK E.M.
25 APRIL 1910

1914 – 1919

H. B. ABEL	J. C. MARSON
P. BALFOUR	J. G. MURDOCH
D. BLYTH	H. V. ORRISS
A. C. CHITTENDEN	R. W. PARKER
L. COULSON	J. C. PARRY
E. CURRY	G. F. PEARSON
R. T. DOSWELL	J. E. RAPHAEL
N. D. EDINBOROUGH	G. W. REED

ST JUDE'S-ON-THE-HILL 217

OPPOSITE The Lady Chapel's mural depicting the Virgin Birth was the first artwork painted by Walter Starmer, who spent a decade decorating the walls and ceilings of the whole church. The wooden statue is a reproduction of the early sixteenth-century 'Mourning Virgin'.

ABOVE The west window, dedicated in 1937, depicts St Jude holding the Cross in his right hand and the church in his left. It was created both in celebration of the church's completion in 1935 and in memory of Basil Graham Bourchier who was vicar from 1908–29.

Holy Trinity

SLOANE STREET, SW1

Three sides of Holy Trinity are constructed of very plain red brickwork, albeit with quite elegant window tracery, but the western front facing out onto Sloane Street is an entirely different matter. The striped polychromatic façade continues the use of red brick but alternates it with lines of pale cream Bath stone, a colour scheme that ultimately blended in harmoniously with the stylish nineteenth-century brick houses and mansion blocks of flats being built in a rapidly expanding Chelsea. The architect chosen for this task was the very artistically minded John Dando Sedding (1838–91), whose career began as a pupil of George Edmund Street and was clearly influenced by Street's eclectic style as his own work developed. The 'outskirts' of London had developed so rapidly from the early nineteenth century that an Act of Parliament was passed to allow the building of many additional churches to serve the increasing population. The Government Commissioners responsible for facilitating those laws purchased the land needed for Holy Trinity from Lord Cadogan in 1821. Plans for that first church were drawn up but its estimated cost was rejected and the pause button pressed for six years. The plans and budget subsequently produced by the architect James Savage were agreed upon and work finally started in 1828. That new church had originally been intended as a chapel of ease for St Luke's Church in Chelsea, but the splitting of that large parish was approved by the Commissioners in 1831 and it was from then that Holy Trinity became a parish church in its own right rather than simply being a 'journey saver'.

There were never any absolutely clear reasons why that new church survived for only half a century, although from the outset there was apparently criticism of its slightly jumbled mélange of Gothic architecture. In the summer of 1888, demolition began and the site cleared for work to begin on the current Sloane Street church of Holy Trinity. One of the most likely reasons for this architectural and spiritual transition was the increasing support for the rapidly emerging Tractarian, Oxford High Church Movement that brought the previous, more symbolic Catholic way of conducting services and Gothic church architecture back into the limelight. It was also probable that Lord Cadogan's high-ranking roles in both the military and political spheres had brought him into contact with many others in the upper echelons of society who were actively supporting that new approach to religious ceremony. Whatever influences affected Lord Cadogan, he willingly gave £20,000 (approx. £3 million today) for the building of a new church, and its ceremonial corner stone was laid by his wife Beatrix, Countess Cadogan, on 30 May 1889.

When one passes through the elegant street-side black iron railings embossed with gold-painted vine leaves and into the main body of the church, the building's structure is not simply an exact replica of one of the three Gothic styles. What the imposing high pillars and arches do provide is support and framing for the intricate artistic elements that together

---

The parish of Holy Trinity is set in an exclusive part of London between Chelsea and Knightsbridge, with several streets and squares in the church's vicinity bearing the name Cadogan. They represent the noble family of George, 5th Earl of Cadogan (1840–1907), who funded and supported the building of the church.

combine to present what Sir John Betjeman, founder of the Victorian Society and Poet Laureate, rightly dubbed as the 'Cathedral of the Arts & Crafts movement'. The east window is the work of two of the movement's highest profile artists, Edward Burne-Jones and William Morris. To say that it is a complex structure might be an understatement, as its lower section comprises forty-eight individual portraits of saints and the upper segments are from the life and death of Christ, interspersed with intricate foliage. The window was the largest ever made by the glaziers Morris & Co., and the saddest thing was that the church's architect, John Dando Sedding, died prematurely from a savage bout of pneumonia that resulted in him not being able to see that most impressive east window in situ. Fortunately, the progress towards the church's completion was neither affected nor diminished by the architect's death, as his talented assistant and successor, Henry Wilson, seamlessly continued the artistic embellishment of this great church.

Many London churches were either demolished or seriously damaged through Second World War bombing raids and Holy Trinity suffered two attacks. One caused damage to the roof that subsequently took ten years to replace, and the organ was so badly damaged that it did not play again for six years. As the organ was set in the choir at the church's east end, it was truly a miracle that the great Arts & Crafts east window was unharmed and remained intact.

OPPOSITE The east window may be the most eye-catching part of the church, but it is surrounded by other notable artworks, such as the carved figures along the organ chamber, the heavily decorated choir stalls, and a truly magnificent chancel gate and rails by Henry Wilson.

ABOVE The reredos is set between the altar and east window and was the work of the Scottish-born artist John Tweed. It is divided into three sections with the central one depicting the Crucified Christ flanked by St John the Baptist and the Virgin and Child.

222 Great Churches of London

ABOVE The bronze angel lectern stood on a red marble dais by the Lady Chapel is undoubtedly one of the stars of the Arts & Crafts portfolio of Holy Trinity, created by H.H. Armstead, a sculptor who had worked with Sir George Gilbert Scott on the Albert Memorial.

OPPOSITE A sequence of windows entitled Virtue, Youth and Charity created by Sir William Blake Richmond is set in the north aisle. All three were donated by Lord Cadogan, and this 'Youth' image was in memory of his son, the Viscount Chelsea, who died in 1878 at the age of twelve.

St Mary Abbots

KENSINGTON CHURCH STREET, W8

St Mary Abbots' name can be traced back to the post-Norman Conquest era when the lord of the manor's son, Godfrey de Vere, fell dangerously ill but was saved by Faritius, Abbot of the Benedictine Abbey of St Mary in Abingdon. As a token of gratitude, the village church and 109 hectares (270 acres) were donated to the abbey, and that connection explains how the word 'Abbots' arrived. During the post Reformation era, that once tiny village began to be occupied by nobility and wealthy Londoners as the City expanded. Its population grew even more when King William III (r. 1689–1702) chose Kensington for his own residence and to house the Royal Court. The Kensington church may have welcomed members of the royal families, generations of local families and well-known people such as William Wilberforce, Sir Isaac Newton and William Makepeace Thackeray, but it really was beyond restoration.

It was in 1868 that Sir George Gilbert Scott (1811–78), a leading architect of the period, was commissioned to design a new church, and it was built in his favourite Gothic Revival style between 1869–72. The vicar at that time was Archdeacon Sinclair and he stated in the first of many fund-raising letters that the new church had to be 'exceedingly magnifical'. The church authorities had initially thought that their new church should be built adjacent to the existing one and north of the churchyard, but Scott suggested that the present site was 'hardly to be passed for convenience and grandeur of position'. He was absolutely right and the church has always been an integral part of Kensington at the junction of High Street and Church Street. Its presence is certainly enriched by the elegant spire that soars to a height of 85m (278ft), making it London's tallest church.

The main formal entry to the church is via the west door, and Scott made it similar to the portal of St Mary's Cathedral in Edinburgh, which he was working on at the same time. The south entrance is far more intriguing and is accessed from an expanse of pavement around the junction of Kensington Church and High Streets. A line of glorious black iron railings runs down the slope of Church Street and ends at a sturdy metal gate. When that gate is open, a vaulted and illuminated pathway like a monastic cloister is the route up to the south door. This was added in 1889–90 and is probably the most atmospheric route into a church one could encounter, though Scott might not have agreed. Although access into the church via the south door is an enchanting way to go, entry via the west portal really enhances one's initial view of the church and it really is most impressive.

The vast, cathedral-like space could easily have been dark and foreboding, but Scott's use of double lancet clerestory windows drops daylight down into the heart of the nave. The proportions of the church are measured at 55m (180ft) long and 33m (108ft) wide and can accommodate over 1,000 worshippers at major festivals such as Christmas. When viewed from the far end of the nave, the distant altar and reredos are well lit, and with every step closer one takes,

---

The beautiful cloister and south porch were the final additions to the church between 1889–93. Unlike a monastic version that is an unbroken loop enabling peaceful prayer and contemplation, St Mary's version simply connects the church with Kensington High Street and the traffic noise.

the quality of the design and materials become even more visually captivating. The reredos was designed by Sir George Gilbert Scott and executed by Clayton & Bell, who were also responsible for the design and creation of the east windows that depict the Nativity, death and Resurrection of Christ.

As one walks up the nave's central aisle en route to the altar, the next noteworthy feature is the hexagonal pulpit created from meticulously carved oak. It was thought to have been given to St Mary Abbots by William III and Queen Mary as they lived just round the corner in Kensington Palace, the main residence for the royal family during that period. To the right of the high altar lies the Resurrection Chapel, created in 1921 by Sir George Gilbert Scott's grandson Giles. It was originally dedicated to those who lost their lives in the First World War. However, that has now been upgraded to include all those connected with the parish who were not just killed in both World Wars but in all other conflicts as well. That south transept housing the war memorials also has a small 'Royal Door' for discreet entry and exit for any member of the royal family attending a service or event.

OPPOSITE: TOP LEFT The Resurrection Chapel altar. TOP RIGHT Elaborately carved choir stalls made from imported Baltic oak. BOTTOM The Resurrection Chapel featuring an angel carved by Queen Victoria's daughter, Princess Louise, in memory of her brothers Alfred (d. 1900) and Leopold (d. 1884).

ABOVE The reredos portrays the four Evangelists in rich mosaics either side of the central cross. St John is seen holding a goblet containing a small green dragon alluding to the Cup of Sorrow foretold by Jesus.
OVERLEAF The High Altar and reredos of St Mary Abbots.

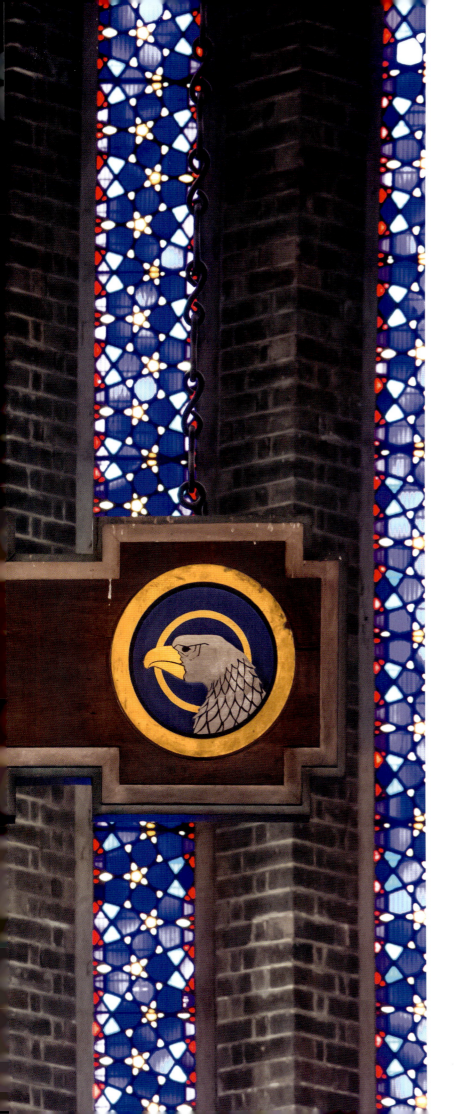

TWENTIETH CENTURY

Second Church of Christ, Scientist

PALACE GARDENS TERRACE, W8

The Second Church of Christ, Scientist is on Palace Gardens Terrace, just off Notting Hill Gate, and occupies a large site comprising substantial red brick buildings whose ecclesiastical history can be traced back to the mid-nineteenth century. The oldest part of the complex was a Victorian church built in 1861–2 under a ninety-year lease to serve the Notting Hill Gate community. Although the first minister was nominally a Baptist, the chapel basically functioned as a non-denominational place of worship for a couple of decades. The next occupants of the chapel were the Swedenborgians, a religious group founded under the theology of Emanuel Swedenborg (1688–1772) and who established it as The New Jerusalem Church. That group was just one of the very many religious organizations that sprang up during the First and Second Great Awakenings originating from the mid-eighteenth century. They all had their own independent views on how Christianity was allegedly failing, who was responsible and what needed to be done to get it all back in line.

The somewhat different philosophy of Christian Science was established in 1879 in Boston, Massachusetts, USA by Mary Baker Eddy (1821–1910). It was a Bible-based religion resting solely upon the teachings of Jesus and the Bible's entire contents from Genesis to Revelation. The founder was apparently healed of a life-threatening injury in 1866 while reading the Bible, thereafter providing her with a fresh insight into how Jesus healed. She went on to describe her personal biblical views and those of others with whom she had made contact and seen their recovery from illness through the Bible. Mary continued to share and verify her discovery, and continued teaching others to heal to such an extent that, in 1875, she went on to publish her major work, *Science and Health with Key to the Scriptures*. Just four years later she established the Church of Christ, Scientist, in Boston, and, two years before her death, launched *The Christian Science Monitor*, an international newspaper that thus far has been the recipient of seven Pulitzer Prizes.

The original Palace Gardens Terrace chapel had actually been able to accommodate a thousand worshippers, but the New Jerusalem Church group had been unable to make that work, and so in 1911 it was sold to the Christian Scientists. Rather than simply revamping the original chapel, the new owners engaged the architects Sir John Burnet & Partners to create a new place of worship adjacent to the existing building. By the time all the plans and legalities had been dealt with, the First World War had begun and everything was temporarily suspended. The new site comprised two buildings, a hall that was completed by 1923, and the church itself followed just three years later. One of the architectural firm's leading designers was the Scottish-born Thomas S. Tait (1882–1954), renowned for designing such Art Deco architectural gems as the *Daily Telegraph*'s Fleet Street building.

The new buildings were adjoined to the original one and the Second Church of Christ, Scientist is the largest part of

---

Every member of the congregation has a clear view of the raised platform, and the acoustics of the church and its impressive organ are just perfect. There is usually a combination of formal services and then smaller groups that gather to discuss biblical and social issues. PREVIOUS PAGES St Saviour's, Eltham.

that L-shaped grouping, with its main entrance facing the road. A large garden area flanked by trees is a useful facility for the junior school now occupying part of the old chapel, and probably also for children attending the Sunday School while their parents are at worship in the church. The main façade facing directly onto Palace Gardens Terrace is a panoply of architectural features with two massive stone columns plus capitals soaring up between the central arch of the large triple window. In a symmetrically perfect grouping, two sets of replica arched windows are down near street level and provide daylight for the church office, library and reading room. The brickwork on the church front represents a beautifully structured façade due to the thinness and subtle tonal variations of the bricks.

The church interior is truly impressive in its design and presentation, with three sides of steeply raked floors all focused down onto the main platform adorned with Art Deco-style furniture. The main feature is the organ whose pipes are harmoniously framed by a wooden structure of the same design and colour as the official chairs set upon the stage.

ABOVE The main body of the church is universally mellow, with both metallic and wood fixtures and furnishings having the same tonal values. Nothing is distracting but everything is visually appealing and very much representative of the Art Deco period in which it was designed.

OPPOSITE: TOP LEFT An elegantly designed window illuminates the rear of the auditorium. TOP RIGHT One of the Art Deco doors on the main platform. BOTTOM LEFT One of the three official chairs on the auditorium's platform. BOTTOM RIGHT Monthly journals for reference in the reading room.

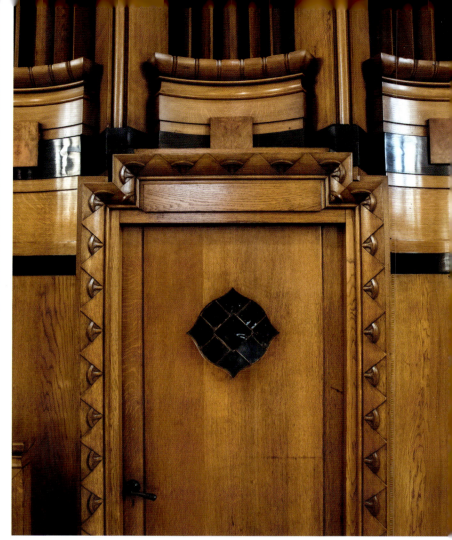

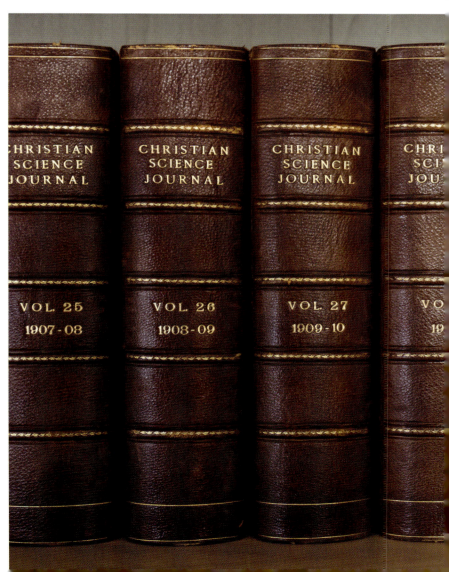

St Saviour

ELTHAM, SE9

The London Borough of Eltham lies to the south-east of Greenwich and is noted for being where the ancient Royal Palace of Eltham was established and Henry VIII spent many of his early years. The palace fell into serious decay and disrepair during the later centuries until 'rescued' in 1933 by the millionaires Stephen and Virginia Courtauld who built an Art Deco house that incorporated the palace's great hall. The landscape around the palace served as royal hunting grounds and each area was given a title relating to its location. Middle Park is just a short distance away and that area was converted into a large housing estate in the early 1930s. Middle Park is now home to around 10,000 people and their spiritual needs were provided for during that same period through the building of St Saviour's. It was one of twenty-five churches commissioned by the Southwark diocese to cater for the rapidly growing number of suburban congregations.

The church was designed by the architect Nugent Francis Cachemaille-Day (1896–1976). He had formed a partnership with Felix Lander and Herbert Welch in 1928, but even during that time had been the primary church designer in the practice. Shortly after the completion of St Saviour's the partnership was dissolved and he reverted back to independency. He became renowned for his 'fortresses' and other large churches whose design veered sharply away from the traditional format. Every church still had to possess a nave, chancel, altar, font and pulpit, and Cachemaille-Day fulfilled those obligations but in an architecturally radical way that has left a visually captivating design signature in many of his sixty-plus churches. He had also previously worked with H.S. Goodhard-Rendel, an architect becoming known for his pared-down Gothic church influences, and those aspects, combined with contemporary German Expressionist and Scandinavian designs, launched Cachemaille-Day into creating his own much acclaimed churches.

Initially, St Saviour's must have seemed even more imposing as many of the surrounding streets would have initially been devoid of trees. The vast church of purple brick with a shallow concrete roof was built in 1932 and upon completion awarded the RIBA (Royal Institute of British Architects) gold medal for its design. The external purple brickwork has a slight change of tone two-thirds of the way up that almost gives the impression of a tidemark. In actual fact, water issues for the church started from the top and worked their way down due to poor drainage. In order to maintain the church's visually unblemished external lines, the architect had designed the roof drainpipes to flow down the interior route and consequently serious damp problems ensued over time. Heritage and Lottery Grants have already been received to combat those issues but such a monumental structure will invariably need further help throughout future decades. Such an important milestone as St Saviour's should receive as much help as possible to enable it to remain a three-dimensional example of architectural design history rather than just a leaf in a book.

The fortress-like church of St Saviour was built in the heart of a new 1930s housing estate in Eltham. It was nicknamed 'the prison' by some locals but the majority welcomed the fact that their community had been endowed with such an impressive church.

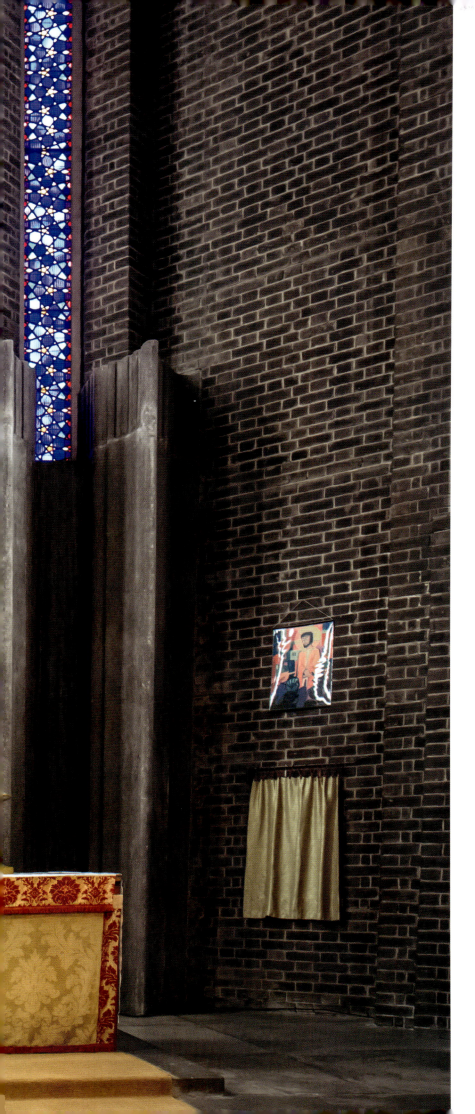

ST SAVIOUR 239

The church interior is so much lighter than one might have imagined due to the north and south walls having been painted white. Reinforced concrete, brickwork and stone are also the interior's main elements, with both the pulpit and lectern being made from bricks, and the massive font at the church's west end is a solid block of concrete with a bowl set into it. The starkness of the font is alleviated by a beautiful carved portrayal of the Baptism of Christ by St John the Baptist on the front face. Set directly above the font is the west end organ and choir gallery, and from that vantage point one can gain an unbroken view of the dramatic and visually compelling elements of the chancel. In contrast to the nave walls, the chancel reverts back to the exterior brick colour and is pierced by four slim blue windows. The reredos itself is created from concrete and dominated by the large central figure of Christ created by the sculptor Donald Hastings (1900–38).

One interesting amendment to the original layout is the 1970s enclosure of the Lady Chapel set on the north side of the chancel. In a church with such a vast interior, it must have been a welcome transition, enabling people to savour personal privacy and tranquillity. St Saviour's inevitably received criticism from many quarters and that is quite understandable given the date of its completion. However, it also became acknowledged as a valuable stepping-stone along the twentieth-century's religious architectural route.

The colour scheme of the high altar and its carpeted shallow steps is an aesthetically perfect contrast to the grey brick surroundings of the chancel. The huge figure of Christ is depicted holding the world in one hand while blessing it with the other.

ST SAVIOUR 241

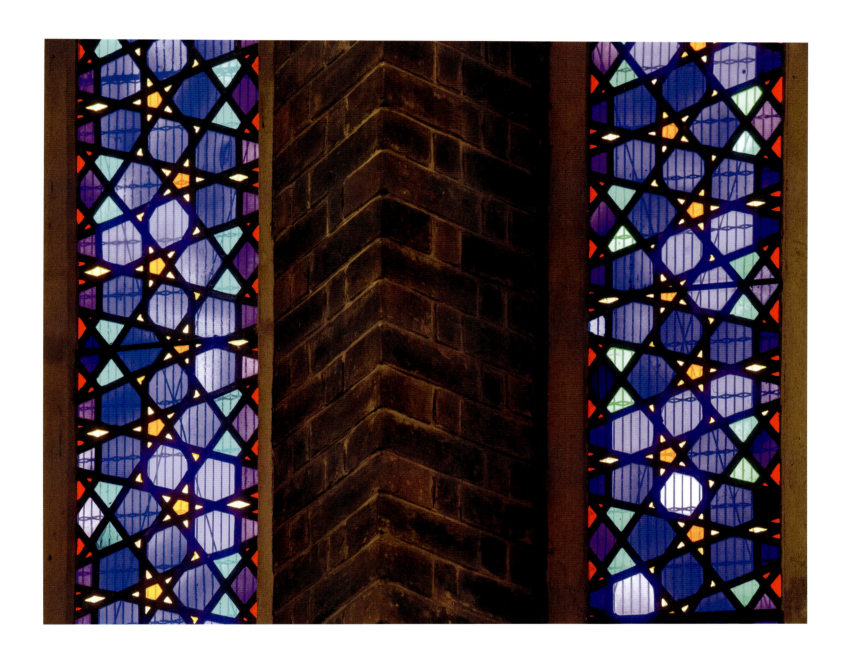

OPPOSITE The chancel comprises a palette of soft colours, thereby combating the harshness of its immediate surroundings. One altar is set at the head of the nave and the high altar rises up above a shallow set of carpeted steps. From the ceiling hangs a strongly coloured cross in gold, red, black and silver.

ABOVE Set into the east wall are two pairs of tall, slender windows filled with intensely glowing patterned glass predominantly in vivid shades of blue. That chancel wall actually rises up to a height of 14m (46ft), significantly greater than intended due to the omission of a proposed room to be set above the altar.

Notre Dame de France

LEICESTER PLACE, WC2

Leicester Square is one of London's main entertainment centres for both tourists and residents, as it is endowed with several major cinemas, casinos, restaurants, and is also on the fringes of 'noodle heaven' in Chinatown. The wide walkway of Leicester Place links the Chinese restaurants of Lisle Street with the Square itself, but as people meander down past a cinema, theatre and ticket office, they will suddenly pass by blue metal gates, railings and a door all covered in small gold crosses. The slightly concave brick façade in which the entrance lies is topped by a dramatic sculpture of the Virgin and Child, with the ledge above adorned with flags from many nations.

That distinctive façade of Notre Dame's entrance leads into a completely circular building that was not built as a place of worship but was actually a form of late eighteenth-century visual entertainment called the 'Burford Panorama'. It was literally a circular building completely covered inside by murals offering unique views of London and other places to customers who stood on viewing platforms to admire the 360-degree panoramas. When the building's lease was about to expire in 1861, Cardinal Wiseman, Archbishop of Westminster, requested that the Marist Fathers (Society of Mary) established a church for the French community in London. He not only acquired the rotunda itself but also managed to purchase another dwelling in Leicester Place, the building subsequently transformed into the current entrance. It all happened during a period when the area now called Chinatown was occupied by significant numbers of French immigrants, so in that latter part of the nineteenth century it was actually 'Frenchtown'.

In 1865, the French architect Louis Auguste Boileau (1812–96) was commissioned to create the church, and at that time was a significant believer in the benefits of cast iron architecture. When it was consecrated in 1868, Notre Dame de France was the first London church to be actually built from cast iron. However, not even solid cast iron structures could totally withstand high explosives and the church was substantially damaged by two bombs in November 1940. Although the church did manage to open temporarily after that disaster, it was not until 1948 that plans were approved for the rebuilding, and a foundation stone from Chartres Cathedral was eventually laid in an official ceremony on 31 May 1953.

Two and a half years later the church received its official consecration in the presence of the Archbishop of Paris, although at that time the issue of the interior's decor still needed to be addressed. The French cultural attaché at that time, René Varin, instigated a campaign that would honour France by adorning the sacred space of Notre Dame with works of art from that period's eminent artists.

The graphically carved bas-relief sculpture of Our Lady of Mercy set high above the main entrance was created by the renowned sculptor Georges-Laurent Saupique (1889–1961), who at that time was also head of the Reims Cathedral restoration. On either side of the main entrance are two

---

The main façade of Notre Dame de France is adorned with graphic sculptures from French artists. The slightly concave brick wall bears a dramatic portrayal of the Virgin, and equally dramatic scenes from her life were carved by French students on both entrance columns.

NOTRE DAME DE FRANCE 245

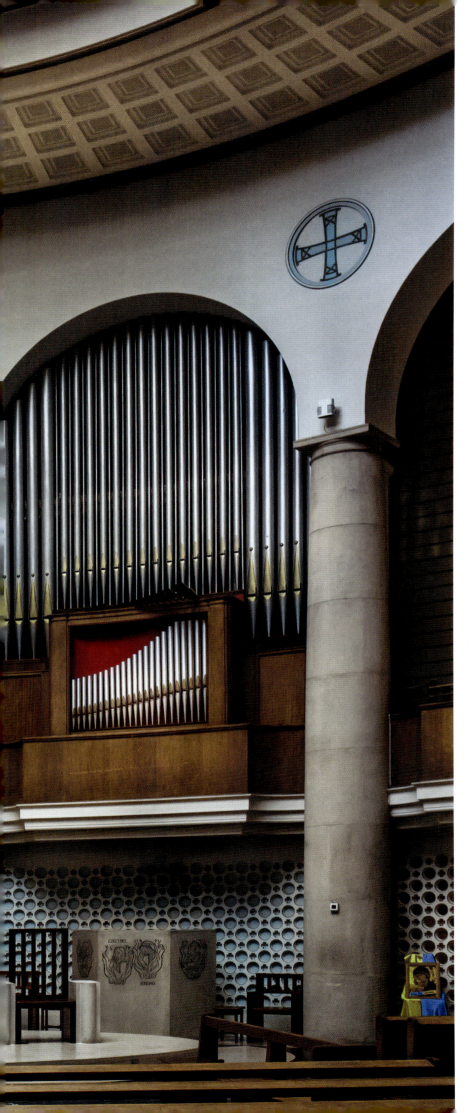

complexly carved pillars by students from the École des Beaux-Arts portraying eight scenes from the life of Mary.

As one enters through the main door, the interior is visually impressive, with twelve Doric columns supporting the gallery and glass-domed roof that floods the interior with daylight. The immediate eye-catching feature lies directly ahead and, although the church may be circular, the layout is based on a rectangular design with symmetrical rows of pews facing straight down to the altar. Set above the altar is a large Aubusson tapestry created in 1954 by the Benedictine monk Dom Robert (Guy de Chaunac-Lanzac, 1907–97). The major theme of his works was pristine Nature, as it emerged from the hands of the Creator, and the beautiful young lady in this tapestry was thought to be Mary being portrayed as the 'New Eve'.

To the left of the altar lies the Mary Chapel, and it was there that the artistic 'star of the show' was created by the legendary artist, poet, playwright and filmmaker Jean Cocteau (1889–1963). He spent just over a week creating the three artworks depicting the Annunciation, Crucifixion and the Assumption of the Virgin Mary. He would arrive each day, light a candle of love and respect, and create what would be his only murals in the United Kingdom. The images may be simply outlined but are truly graphic in their interpretation of those three climactic events in the Christian World. Cocteau was so famous that he had to be protected by hastily erected screens to prevent crowds intruding on his workplace.

The church of Notre Dame de France was created from a circular, late eighteenth-century Panorama, and instead of portraying dramatic landscapes and 360-degree views of London, it is now endowed with a captivating portfolio of art and sculpture created mainly by French artists.

246 GREAT CHURCHES OF LONDON

ABOVE The Aubusson tapestry set above the altar was the work of Dom Robert, a Benedictine monk renowned for his works. The theme is Paradise on Earth and portrays the 'New Eve' (a title given to Mary by the Church) in the midst of Nature.

OPPOSITE: TOP Jean Cocteau's portrayal of the Crucifixion was one of the graphic and unique Lady Chapel artworks he created in gratitude for being awarded an honorary doctorate from Oxford University. BOTTOM A mosaic depicting Mary and the newly born Jesus by Russian artist Boris Anrep.

Most Holy Trinity

DOCKHEAD, SE1

The Most Holy Trinity is the imposing and truly majestic Grade II*-listed church located on Dockhead, just about 400m (¼ mile) downstream from Tower Bridge and even closer to where the underground river Neckinger surfaces to enter the Thames at the historic St Saviour's Dock. That entry point was originally developed by the Cluniac monks of nearby Bermondsey Abbey to facilitate a safe landing place for both bishops and goods. It later descended into an area so steeped in crime, poverty and disease that it featured as home for the villains of Charles Dickens' *Oliver Twist*. That historic area of St Saviour's and the neighbouring cobbled street of Shad Thames are now largely comprised of blocks of warehouses converted into exclusive and expensive apartments, but it was also the area where the violent anti-Catholic Gordon Riots of 1780 took place. It was just two years after the passing of the Papists Act of 1778, intended to reduce official discrimination again Catholics, but head of the Protestant Association, Lord George Gordon, had apparently decreed that it would enable Catholics to join the British Army and plot treason.

Dockhead's religious heritage can be traced back to that eighteenth-century period when its first established chapel was destroyed in those riots. The place of worship eventually built as a replacement during the early Victorian period was the very large, galleried Most Holy Trinity church in the Early English Gothic style. Despite its potentially perilous location close by the Thames, it survived the Blitz but, just two months before the end of the Second World War, a V-2 rocket exploded close by and caused massive damage. Many of London's churches had already been destroyed but few had adjoining priest's houses, vicarages and convents in the manner of Dockhead's. It was there that three priests were instantly killed and another plus the housekeeper were still alive but buried in the rubble. A diminutive local milkman, also working with the Heavy Rescue Squad, volunteered to crawl through the rubble and facilitate their rescue and was subsequently awarded the George Cross medal for his bravery. That outstanding humanitarian act united the parish and strengthened its desire to recover and rebuild.

The replacement Most Holy Trinity Church now dominating the junction of Dockhead and Jamaica Road was designed and built in 1957–60 by the renowned architect H.S. Goodhart-Rendel CBE (1887–1959). It was immensely sad that such a talented and much-revered person should die shortly before the completion of his magnificent final church, but at least his successors, F.G. Broadbent and Partners, honoured every aspect of the design. Goodhart-Rendel had a privileged background, went to study music at Cambridge, but later opted to enter the world of architecture. He converted to Catholicism in 1936 and thereafter was engaged in quite a few church projects. One of his great influencers was the famous French Gothic Revival architect Eugène-Emmanuel Viollet-le-Duc (1814–79), responsible for many notable restorations including Notre-Dame de Paris. Most of Holy Trinity's west front definitely has the aura of Medieval

---

The Most Holy Trinity's hexagonal towers make the church really stand out amid the urban landscape. Its site is comparatively clear and so not hemmed in like some London churches, thereby enabling one to marvel at the architect's design and the bricklayers who executed it.

250 Great Churches of London

MOST HOLY TRINITY 251

Romanesque architecture. The sheer solidity of its façade flanked by twin towers and a huge west window set above the main entrance is definitely an example of successfully winding back the architectural clock a few centuries. The complexity of the three-toned brickwork is astounding, and if one ever gets chance to visit, stand below the south front with its vast clear light windows and intricate brick patterns as it really is an impressive piece of work.

The fascinating thing about this church is that the moment one steps into the nave, there is little visual continuity in terms of the architectural period. Yes, there may be arches and other features that could be linked to the Gothic era, but even so, the contrast between the interior and exterior design and use of differing materials is very much the hallmark of Goodhart-Rendel. The nave appears quite narrow due to the fact that the flanking aisles are now corridors set behind nave walls and the semi-circular stone pulpit is accessed via stairs set in the north aisle. The layout and delicate colouring of the nave is designed to ensure worshippers' eyes are focused on the altar, which itself is surrounded on three sides by richly panelled stonework. The architect acquired stone, slate and timber from sources throughout Britain to ensure that every single part of the church would combine to create a portfolio of visual harmony, and the sheer size, design and vibrancy of Most Holy Trinity has resulted in a truly remarkable landmark.

The chancel is a beautifully designed combination of colours and textures, all well lit due to the absence of stained glass. A gilded mahogany canopy is placed above the original high altar and the forward-facing altar of white marble is now clearly visible to every member of the congregation.

252 GREAT CHURCHES OF LONDON

The church is adorned with a most beautifully created collection of high relief glazed ceramic images for its traditional Catholic Stations of the Cross. They were created by the London-based sculptor Atri Cecil Brown (1906–82) and added to the church's south aisle in 1971.

MOST HOLY TRINITY 253

Atri Cecil Brown also created the triptych set above the original high altar, now redundant for High Mass since the 1960s Vatican II revisions determined that it should be conducted facing the congregation. From left to right they depict the Nativity, Christ with St Peter and the Pentecost.

St Paul's

BOW COMMON, E3

As its name suggests, in the pre-Victorian era Bow Common was little more than a common grazing ground but, as London expanded, such areas became heavily inhabited and that growing population needed places of worship. The original church dedicated to St Paul was built in 1858 and was a typical urban Victorian church with much stained glass and a huge spire to remind parishioners of its presence. Bow Common rapidly grew into a large industrial area with several gas works supplying the capital's needs. However, during the Blitz of the Second World War in 1941, incendiary bombs virtually gutted the church but fortunately the War Reparation scheme did provide funding for a replacement.

The building of a new church did not happen immediately, and it was not until a decade had elapsed that it started to progress. The creation of the current St Paul's would become a landmark event in the UK's world of religious architecture. In that early post-war period the vicar of the Bow Common parish was Gresham Kirkby (1916–2006), who took up the post in July 1951, and served for over four decades. During the early years, his enthusiasm for the Liturgical Movement would shape the future of the church and parish. That organization was about the merits of simplicity in churches becoming more acceptable to worshippers than the sumptuous aspects of display that featured so heavily in High Church Masses. The Reverend Kirkby had already undertaken a tour of Europe to observe how the Liturgical Movement was transforming the divisions between priests and congregation during Mass. He was not overly impressed with what he encountered and, having returned home, made contact with a young architect, Robert Maguire (1931–2019), whose work in a nearby chapel had impressed him. Maguire was also becoming infatuated with the ideology of the Movement, and while working on that particular project had teamed up with another like-minded designer, Keith Murray (1892–1981). As a result of those coincidental encounters they submitted plans for a replacement church to the appropriate authorities. Those drawings were actually based upon an earlier student project completed by Maguire, one that his college tutors almost failed because its brutalist, concrete nature dared to challenge the long-held perceptions of what a church should actually look like.

What Maguire and Murray's church created between 1958–60 did look like was the place of worship still standing today. Their talented approach was eventually rewarded when St Paul's was awarded a Grade II* listing in 1988, and its architectural and artistic value was further recognized in 2013, when it won first prize in the 'Post 1953' category of a competition held by the National Churches Trust.

The most important element of the Liturgical Movement was the altar's placement within the heart of the nave, thereby breaking down physical barriers between the worshippers and the Celebrant of the Eucharist. The seating was also a key issue, and the very flexible way that the easily manhandled benches could be arranged further minimized the formality. There are few windows and most of the natural light floods down from the large diamond-shaped lantern contrasting

A passing glance at St Paul's might initially suggest a curious brick box, but it rightly received architectural awards that saw its creators rewarded with the accolades they deserved for this piece of creative genius.

aesthetically well with the brick and concrete. The other notable exterior feature is the dramatic carved lettering created by Ralph Beyer (1921–2008), who had been taught by the great sculptor Henry Moore and worked to transform lettering from being a craft tradition into an art form. He created the lintels around the entrance porch by first designing each letter and then imprinting each one into the wet concrete. He chose a statement from the Book of Genesis that extends around the three sides and reads 'Truly this is none other but the House of God, this is the Gate of Heaven'.

The interior walls are cleverly softened by another sublime work of art that was thought to be Britain's largest single mosaic designed and executed by one person. That artist was Charles Lutyens (1933–2021), great-nephew of the famous architect Edwin Lutyens, and his project was entitled 'Angels of the Heavenly Host', an artwork that took him five years to complete. The tiles were accessed from the Venetian island of Murano, and his chosen palette was finally comprised of 700 colours. The mural depicted twelve angels with one of the four Elements in each corner. Yes, there may be architectural elements of bleakness in the design and construction of St Paul's, but it is aesthetically beautiful if one just refocuses the mind away from what churches were always allegedly supposed to look like.

BELOW Charles Lutyens spent five years making the angel mosaics that completely encircle the walls. Just study this image and try to imagine what a task it must have been to work on day after day after day.

OPPOSITE The sense of 'family' was created by following the Liturgical Movement principles and moving the high altar into the heart of the church so that the priest was not seemingly aloof or detached from his parishioners.

Lumen United Reformed Church

TAVISTOCK PLACE, WC1

Set in the heart of Bloomsbury, Tavistock Place is lined with rows of elegant Georgian terraced houses, which at one point are interrupted by the stunning new Lumen United Reformed Church and Community Centre. The creation of the United Reformed Church in 1972 when the Presbyterian Church of England and the Congregational Church in England and Wales merged into one religious body. That denomination was further expanded just a few years later when joined by the Churches of Christ in 1981 and the Scottish Congregationalists in 2000. The original Gothic-style church with twin towers closely resembling York Minster had been established in the nearby Regent Square in 1827. It was during the latter months of the Second World War that the church and accompanying halls were so badly damaged by a V-2 rocket that crucial decisions about reconstruction had to be made. It took many years of negotiation with the War Damage Commission before a grant was accepted in 1958, and the new church was built and eventually opened in 1966. Four decades later, the architectural partnership of Theis and Khan was commissioned to completely redesign and restructure the building.

As one approaches the church, there is a discreet sign bearing the word 'Lumen' and a brown wooden cross fixed onto the brick frontage. A large proportion of the street front's façade is actually taken up by a fascinating 8-m (26-ft) high window, providing some detail from outside, but as soon as one crosses the threshold its true complex structure is revealed. It was the work of Rona Smith and entitled 'North Elevation', a complex bronze sculpture curving gently into the church derived from the sacred geometry found in Hindu and Islamic traditions. Having grasped and admired its design, one's eyes are immediately diverted into the church interior where a gigantic white conical sphere pierces the centre of the room. It was another creative master-stroke by the architects, and the 11-m (36-ft) high 'shaft of light' drops down from a hole in the ceiling into a space dividing the café and area of worship. The light floods down onto the enclosed floor space that is furnished with a few chairs and floor cushions so that anyone seeking peace, tranquillity and contemplation can just hide away from the stress and bustle of life outside.

The third artistic masterpiece in this one room is the stained glass window designed by Pierre Fourmaintraux and installed in 1966. It was such a prized piece of art that it was removed from its original setting and relocated into its current position. It was created in a technique referred to as *dalle de verre* ('slab of glass') and comprises 1,000 pieces of 2.5cm (1in) thick glass in twenty-one panels. Every segment was cut by scoring the glass and hitting it with a hammer on a small anvil to ensure a clean break. The surface of the glass was then slightly chipped to ensure that sunlight hitting it goes in all directions. The fragments of glass were then set in concrete that was reinforced, vibrated and set to make a resilient and secure frame. Had it not been used, it is unlikely that the window would have been able to leave its original location

---

The elegant brick-built Georgian houses on Tavistock Place were joined in 1966 by the Lumen United Reformed Church that was originally established just round the corner but relocated after the Second World War. The vast window adorning the front façade is a truly magnificent piece of artwork.

260 GREAT CHURCHES OF LONDON

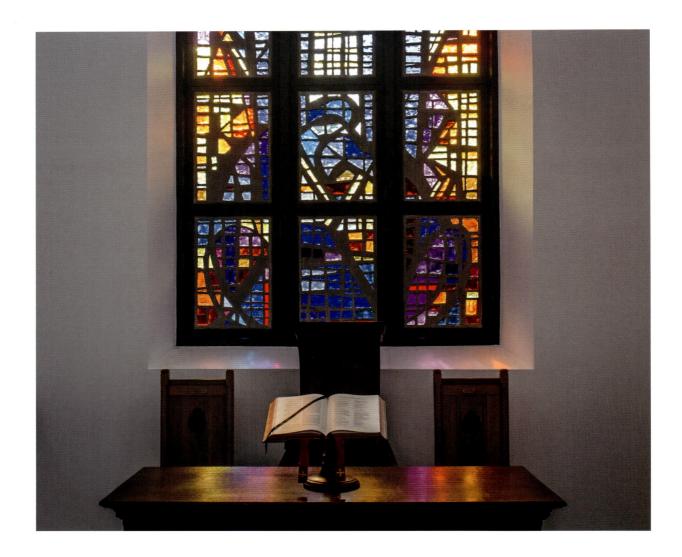

in one piece. It represents the Resurrection and from the top down shows Christ risen from the Tomb carrying the flag of a red cross on a white background, and the bowed figure of Mary surrounded by spears.

Alison Wilding was another artist commissioned to provide essential elements, and created a stunningly beautiful new font, a drinking fountain and also an outdoor fountain. That area was created from the original church car park, and its courtyard garden is beautifully planted with silver birch and other shrubs, and furnished with chairs and tables, all of which are encircled by a path in true cloisters fashion. There are also three community rooms available for hire and a gallery space for local artists. Lumen is close to several colleges, King's Cross, Euston and St Pancras stations, and its current mode is a perfect one to cater for personal religious needs and both business and social events.

All those elements are there to offer help, comfort and facilities to anybody, regardless of their religion or nationality, and the United Reformed Church is spread widely across England, Wales and Scotland. The quality of architecture, art and craftsmanship in this current Lumen church certainly makes it feel as though nothing other than prayer and pastoral care will be needed for a very long time.

ABOVE The place of worship inside the church is backed by a dramatic piece of glass comprising 1,000 pieces individually cut and set in concrete. There is a narrative set within the glass, but relating that to the image itself can be quite tricky.

OPPOSITE A substantial part of the church's interior is taken up by the white conical mass that tapers up until it pierces the ceiling. It is not as solid as it looks but is actually a hollow 'sacred place' furnished with chairs and cushions.

St Mary's

BARNES, SW13

Just a couple of weeks before the longest day of summer on 8 June 1978, the village of Barnes was subjected to the horror of the longest night for many residents as they watched their beloved parish church blaze into potential oblivion. When the blue flashing lights and pumps of the fire engines were finally turned off and the extent of the nightmare was revealed, opinions were divided as to whether or not it could possibly be rescued and renovated, or whether demolition and rebuilding was the only solution. Perhaps the most extraordinary thing was that the Tudor period tower emerged virtually unscathed and some of the church's other older parts were not reduced to rubble. As St Mary's had a history extending back many centuries, it was hoped that some kind of rebuilding programme might be considered.

The church actually dates back to the early or mid-twelfth century when a simple rectangular chapel dedicated to the Virgin Mary was erected to serve the sparsely populated Thames-side village of Barnes. The most significant part of the church left partially intact after the fire was the medieval east end chapel that was added during the early thirteenth century. It was around that time that Archbishop Stephen Langton was appointed Archbishop of Canterbury (1207–28) during the reign of King John (r. 1199–1216), and he was a significant contributor in both the drafting and sealing of the famous Magna Carta, signed by King John at Runnymede on the River Thames on 15 June 1215. It was on his way back to London after the signing ceremony in front of all the leading barons that the archbishop stopped off at Barnes to dedicate the church of St Mary. That was recognized by the title subsequently given to the east end chapel rebuilt after the fire that is now known as the Langton Chapel.

That re-creation was one of the easier parts of the designing and reconstruction of the rest of the church. There was an awful lot of wrangling over what should happen, how St Mary's should be redesigned, what should be kept or permanently dismantled, and so on. What actually did happen first was that a team of archaeologists began a detailed survey of the site of the ancient South London parish church. The survey was mostly centred around the oldest parts of the church and it seemed that the later Victorian and Edwardian additions were way beyond repair. All sorts of valuable discoveries were made as the teams carefully worked their way through the rubble, and it was the remains of the south wall that were of significant historical importance. Prior to the fire, the wall had been covered by large stone monuments and memorials to parishioners dating from the seventeenth to the twentieth century. Most had fallen to the ground and dragged several layers of plaster with them, and what was revealed enabled the experts to categorically state that the church stood on the site it had occupied since the start of the twelfth century.

Archive black and white photographs from this time document the complicated part of carefully removing and assessing items that were previously hidden. These included gleaming white skeletons that had to be carefully removed

---

The early thirteenth-century chancel was one of the few surviving features of the original church and has been beautifully restored to retain its atmosphere. The roof is patently new, but the coarse stone walls withstood the flames and have beautiful textures.

ST MARY'S 265

and were then formally reburied in 1981 at a privately held service. Everything recovered from walls, floors and roofs was forensically examined, meticulously recorded and saved for reference or future use in the rebuilding programme.

The great thing about the St Mary rebuilding project was that as many of the original features as possible were restored, retained and in some instances repositioned to make the area more viable as a community church. The architect was Edward Cullinan, and he strove tirelessly to make the church work better. One of the key elements was the removal of the overbearing Victorian nave, enabling a more intimate experience where up to 500 people can sit around the altar on three sides, and that area is now perfectly lit by a new roof lantern. What they achieved via the redesign was exactly the same kind of intimacy and congregational consideration sought by the twentieth-century architects building the new churches such as St Paul's, Bow Common (page 255), reducing the staid formality of their predecessors.

The copious use of wood and warm-toned lighting really does give such a comfortable atmosphere. Hopefully, even parishioners who were originally unenthusiastic about their rebuilt church will have mellowed over the four decades that have now elapsed since its 1984 rehallowing service.

The new interior of St Mary's is a warm and welcoming place. The angled timber roofing sloping down into the nave has created a great acoustic quality. OVERLEAF The brilliant combination of medieval and modern architecture with beautiful red tiled roofing links everything together.

INDEX

Page numbers in *italics* indicate illustration captions.

A
Academy of St Martin-in-the-Fields 111
Adams-Acron, John *128*
All Hallows by the Tower, Byward Street, EC3 30–7
All Saints, Margaret Street, W1 158–63
All Souls, Langham Place, W1 152–6
Allon, Henry 201
Anne, Queen 102–5
Anrep, Boris *246*
Archer, Thomas 102, 123
Armstead, H.H. *222*
Arnold of Nijmegen 119
Art Deco 233, *234*, 236
Artari, Giuseppe 108, *115*
Arts & Crafts 24, 194, *198*, 221, 222
Aubusson 245, *246*

B
Bagutti, Giovanni 108, *115*
Barnett, Henrietta 213
Barnett, Samuel 213, *213*
Baroque 6, 102, 123, 124
Bartholomew the Apostle 10, *14*
BBC 152, 155
Bedford, Duke of 99
Bell, Daniel *179*
Beresford-Hope, Alexander 158
Bernini, Gian Lorenzo 92, 123
Betjeman, Sir John 221
Beyer, Ralph 256
Blake, William 128
Blakeman, Charles and May 24
Blitz (1940–1), 6, 10, 19, 30, 39, 67, 81, 206, 242, 248, 255
Boileau, Louis Auguste 242
Bolton, William *13*
Borromini, Francesco 123
Bourchier, Basil Graham *214*
Brown, Atri Cecil *252*, *253*
Brown, Dan *The Da Vinci Code* 19
Bunhill Fields burial site 128
Bunyan, John 128
Burne-Jones, Edward 221
Burnet & Partners, Sir John 233
Butterfield, William 92, *95*, 158, 161

C
Cachemaille-Day, Nugent Francis 236
Cadogan, George, 5th Earl 218, *218*, 222
Catherine, Saint 39
Charles I 39
Charles II *33*
Chavalliaud, Léon-Joseph 149
Christ Church, Spitalfields, Commercial Street, E1 84–89
Church of the Immaculate Conception, Farm Street, W1 170–3
City of London Cemetery, Ilford 91
Classical 39, 85, 91, 96, 116, 140
Clayton & Bell *100*, *145*, 164, 227
Clayton, 'Tubby' 33
Clement, Saint 70
Coade stone 135, *139*, 140
Coade, Eleanor 135
Coal Tax 91, 119
Cocteau, Jean 245, *246*
Comper, Sebastian 206
Comper, Sir John Ninian 158, 161, *161*, *163*, *174*, 206, *206*
Cosmati Pavement, Westminster Abbey 166
Courtauld, Stephen and Virginia 236
Crewe, Lord 213
Croke, John 35
Cubitt, James *201*, 201–3
    Church Design for Congregations 201
Cullinan, Edward 265
Cuthbert, Saint 194

D
Dance, George, the Younger 128
De Vasconcellos, Josefina de *The Risen Christ* *14*
Decorated Period Gothic 194
Defoe, Daniel 128
Diamond, David 124
Dickens, Charles 60, 248
Dissolution of the Monasteries (1536–41) 10, 23, 39
Dom Robert (Chaunac-Lanzac, Guy de) 245, *246*
Dowding, Lord Hugh 73
Dyce, William 161

E
École des Beaux Arts 245
Eddy, Mary Baker 233
Edinburgh, Duke of 70
Edward, Prince of Wales *35*
Edwards, Carl 17, *20*, 73
Eliot, T.S. 'The Waste Land' 49
Elizabeth I 23
Elizabeth II 70, 131
Elizabeth, the Queen Mother 33, 149
England & Russell 81
English Heritage 6, 86, 99, 194
Erectheion, Acropolis, Athens 140, *141*, 142, *142*
Erith, Raymond 149
Erkenwald, Bishop of London 30
Etheldreda, Saint 23

F
F.G. Broadbent and Partners 248
Faber, Frederick William 183, 185
'Fifty Churches Act' (1710) 6, 91, 96, 102, 119
    Commission for Building Fifty New Churches 78, 85, 116, 123
First World War 33, 111, 197, 214, *214*, 227, 233
Fontana, Carlo 102
Foster, John 149
Fourmaintraux, Pierre 258
Francis I, Pope 170
Franklin, Benjamin 10

Franklin, Sir John 132–5
Friends of Christ Church Spitalfields 86
Friends of London Churches 67
Fynes-Clinton, Fr. 49

G
Gambier-Parry, Sidney 188
Gayer, Sir John 40
Geldart, Ernest 197
George I 96, 105, 108, 116
George III 131
George IV 152, *152*, 155
George V 13
Gherkin 39
Gibbons, Grinling 30, *36*, 64, *64*, 67, *119*
Gibbons, Harold *191*
Gibbs, James 70, *70*, 116
    A Book of Architecture 108
    St Clement Danes 70, 102, *102*
    St Martin-in-the-Fields 108, *112*, *115*, 116
    St Mary Le Strand 102–5, 116
Gibson, Edmund 96
Gill, Colin *192*
Gill, Eric *214*
Glaziers Company *20*, 73
Goodhart-Rendel, H. S. 188–91, *191*, 236, 248, 251
Gordon, Lord George 248
Gothic 6, 17, 39, 85, 91, 119, 194, *194*, 218, 236, 251
    Gothic Perpendicular 78, 206
    Gothic Revival 158, 173, 174, 206, 224, 248
Gough, Hugh Roumieu 194
Grant, Charles *100*
Great Fire of London (1966) 6, 10, 23, 30, 33, 39, 52, 55, 59, 64, 70, 78, 91, 123
Greek Cross 52, 59, *60*, 146, *146*
Greek Revival 142, 158, 164, 173
Green, Samuel *139*

Greenwich Hospital Chapel, Greenwich, SE10 *128*, 132–9
Grey, William 64
Gribble, Herbert 183
Grosvenor, Sir Richard 170
Gutch, Charles 206, 209

H
Handel, George Frideric 119
Hanks, Tom 19
Harris, Sir Arthur 'Bomber' 73
Hastings, Donald 239
Hatton, Sir Christopher 23
Hawksmoor, Nicholas 6, 132
    Christ Church, Spitalfields 85–6, 88
    St George's, Bloomsbury Way 96–9
    St Mary Woolnoth 91, *92*, 95
Hendrix, Jimi 119
Henry I 10, 13
Henry III 17
Henry VIII *10*, 19, 23, 39, 108, 123, 170, 213, 236
Heraclius, Patriarch of Jerusalem 17
Heritage Lottery Fund 194, 236
Heron, Patrick 57
Hirst, Damien *Exquisite Pain* 14
Holiday, Henry *177*, 179
Holy Trinity, Sloane Street, SW1X 218–23
Horne, Pip *112*
Houshiary, Shirazeh *112*
Howell, Cyril 188

I
Ignatius of Loyola, Saint 170, 173
Inwood, Henry William 140, 142
Inwood, William 140

J
J.W. Walker & Sons *111*
James I 19
James, John 116
Jesuit Order 170, *171*

John, King 262
Johnson, Samuel 73
Jordan, Abraham 46

K
Keble, Henry 78
Kent, William *The Last Supper* 119
Kirkby, Gresham 255
Kirkpatrick, Richard Carr 164
Knights Templar 6, 17–19

L
Langton, Stephen 262
Laud, William 39
Lavers and Westlake *203*
Lee, Lawrence *81*
London Oratory, Brompton Road, SW7 6, 182–7
Lucchesi, Andrea 198
Lumen United Reformed Church, Tavistock Place, WC1 258–61
Lutyens, Charles *256*, 256
Lutyens, Sir Edwin 213, *213*, 256

M
Magnus, Earl of Orkney 46
Maguire, Robert 255
Margins Project 203
Marshall, Gilbert, 4th Earl of Pembroke 19
Marshall, Joshua 70
Martin, Saint 111
Martin, Richard *20*
Mary, Princess 13
Mary of Teck 108
Mausoleum, Halicarnassus, Turkey 96
Montagu, Duke of 99
Moore, Henry 55, *57*, 256
Morris & Co. 221
Morris, William 221
Most Holy Trinity, Dockhead, SE1 248–53

Mottistone, Lord 30, 33
Murray, Keith 255

N
Nash, John 152, *152*, 155, *155*
National Lottery Fund 6, 86
Nelson, Horatio 108
Neoclassicism 132, 135, *135*, 139
Newman, John Henry 183, *183*
Newton, John 92
Newton, Sir Isaac 224
Newton, William 132, *135*
Normans 6, 10, 30
Notre Dame de France, Leicester Place, WC2 242–7
Nuttgens Edward 24

O
Old Royal Naval College, Greenwich 132
Our Lady of Walsingham, Norfolk 49, *50*

P
Paget, Paul 30
Palumbo, Lord Peter 55
Pancras, Saint 140
Papworth, John *139*
Paul III, Pope 170
Peacock Pluteus Stone 35
Pearce, Edward 70
Pearson, John Loughborough 164, *164*, 166
Penn, William 30
Pepys, Samuel 30
Perpendicular *14*, 33, *33*, 78, 81, 206
Philip IV of France 19
Philip Neri, Saint 183
Plaw, John 146
Plowden, Sir Edward *20*
Polish Air Force 73
Portland stone 123–4, 140, 142
Pugin, Augustus 173

R
Rahere 10, *14*
Reynolds, Sir Joshua 149
Reynolds, William Bainbridge 197, *198*
Richmond, Sir William Blake *222*
Ripley, Thomas 132
Romanesque 6, 10, *13*, 17, *19*, 251
Rossi, J.C.F. 140
Rounthwaite, William 17
Royal Air Force 70–3

S
St Augustine's, Kilburn Park Road, NW6 164–9
St Bartholomew the Great, West Smithfield, EC1 6, 9–15
St Clement Danes, Strand, WC2 70–7, 102, *102*, 108
St Cuthbert's, Philbeach Gardens, SW5 *158*, 194–9
St Cyprian's, Glentworth Street, NW1 206–11
St Etheldreda's, Ely Place 22–9
St George's, Bloomsbury Way, WC1 96–101
St George's, Hanover Square, W1 116–21
St Jude's-on-the-Hill, Hampstead Garden Suburb, NW11 212–17
St Katharine Cree, Leadenhall Street, EC3 38–45
St Magnus the Martyr, Lower Thames Street, EC3 46–51
St Martin-in-the-Fields, Trafalgar Square, WC2 70, 108–15, 116
St Martin-within-Ludgate, Ludgate Hill, EC4 58–63
St Mary Abbots, Kensington Church Street, W8 224–30
St Mary Abchurch, Abchurch Lane, EC4 64–9

St Mary Aldermary, Bow Lane, EC4 78–83
St Mary Le Strand, Strand, WC2 70, 102–7, 108, 116
St Mary Magdalene, Paddington, W2 174–81
St Mary Woolnoth, Lombard Street, EC3 90–5
St Mary's, Barnes, SW13 262–7
St Mary's, Bourne Street, SW1 188–93
St Mary's, Paddington Green, W2 146–51
St Pancras New Church, Euston Road, NW1 140–5
St Paul's Cathedral 6, 52, *59*, 70, 123, 128, *142*
St Paul's Deptford, SE8 122–6
St Paul's, Bow Common, E3 254–57, 265
St Saviour, Eltham, SE9 236–41
St Stephen Walbrook, Walbrook, EC4 52–7
Salviati works *177*
Samaritans 55
Saupique, Georges-Laurent 242
Savage, James 218
scagliola 142
Scarborough, Earl of 170
Scoles, J.J. 170
Scott, Giles 227
Scott, Sir George Gilbert *222*, 224, 227
Second Church of Christ, Scientist, Palace Gardens Terrace, W8 232–40
Second World War 6, 10, 24, 33, 52, *59*, 70, *152*, 155, 194, 221, 248, 255, 258
Sedding, John Dando 218, 221
Seymour, Edward, 1st Duke of Somerset 102
Sheppard, Dick 111
Siddons, Sarah 149, *151*
Sky Garden *30*
Smith, Rona 258

Snow, William 67, *68*
Society of King Charles the Martyr 39, *43*
Spear, Ruskin 70, *77*
Starmer, Walter P. 214, *217*
Stephen, Saint 57
Stewart, William 116
Stott, John 155
Street, G.E. 99
Street, George Edmund 174, 218
Stuart, James 'Athenian' 132, *135*
    Antiquities of Athens 132
Swedenborg, Emanuel 233

T
Tait, Thomas S. 233
Tapisserie 57
Temple Church, Temple, EC4 6, 16–21
Thackeray, William Makepeace 224
Thatcher, Margaret, Carol, and Mark *131*
Theis and Khan 258
Thomas, Brian 36
Throckmorton, Sir Nicholas 40
TocH 33, *35*
Tower of the Winds, Athens 140, *145*
Travers, Martin 46, 46–9, 188, *191*
Tweed, John *221*

U
UNESCO World Heritage Site 132
Union Chapel, Compton Terrace, Islington N1 200–5
United States Air Force 73

V
Van Eyck, Jan *50*
Vanbrugh, John 132
Varah, Chad 55
Varin, René 242
Verde Antico 142
Victoria, Queen 227

Victoria & Albert Museum 99
Viollet-le-Duc, Emmanuel 248

W
War Damage Commission 258
War Reparation 255
Ward & Hughes 88
Ward, Sir Patience 67
Webb, Aston 13
Wesley, Charles 128, 131
Wesley, George 128
Wesley, Susanna 128
Wesley's Chapel, City Road, EC1Y 128–31
    Foundery Chapel 128, 131, *131*
West, Benjamin 135
West, Richard Temple 174, *174*
Westhall, Henry 194–7
Whistler, Rex 185
Wilberforce, William 92, *100*, 224
Wilding, Alison 260
Wilkins, Chrysostom 105
William and Mary 132, 224, 227
William the Conqueror 6, 30, 52, 70
Wilson, Henry 221, *221*
Wiseman, Cardinal 242
Withers, Robert Jewell 188
Women's Royal Naval Service 105
Wood, Henry *163*
World Monuments Fund 99
Wren, Christopher 6, 17, 91, 116, 123, 132, *132*
    St Clement Danes 70
    St Magnus the Martyr 46
    St Martin-within-Ludgate 59, 60
    St Mary Abchurch 64, 67, *67*, *68*
    St Mary Aldermary 78–81
    St Stephen Walbrook 52, 55

Y
York, Duke of 142

Quarto

First published in 2024
by Frances Lincoln,
an imprint of Quarto.
One Triptych Place,
London, SE1 9SH
United Kingdom
T (0)20 7700 6700
www.Quarto.com

Text and photograhs © 2024 Derry Brabbs

All rights reserved. No part of this book may be reproduced or utilized in any form or by any means, electronic or mechanical, including photocopying, recording or by any information storage and retrieval system, without permission in writing from Frances Lincoln.

A catalogue record for this book is available from the British Library.

ISBN 978-0-7112-6923-1
eISBN 978-0-7112-6924-8

10 9 8 7 6 5 4 3 2 1

Commissioning Editor: Philip Cooper
Project Editor: Michael Brunström
Designer: Arianna Osti
Art Director: Isabel Eeles
Production Controller: Eliza Walsh

Printed in China

ACKNOWLEDGEMENTS

My grateful thanks to Arianna Osti for her brilliant design and yet another intuitive final picture selection that perfectly encapsulates the atmosphere, history and architecture of the London Churches.

Sincere thanks also to my publisher, Philip Cooper and editor Michael Brunström from the Frances Lincoln imprint of Quarto Publishing. We may be more reliant upon the latest 'high-tech' mobile phones but even though one can now actually download a whole book, publishers such as Frances Lincoln thankfully still believe that a book is only a book if it has pages to turn rather than scroll.

I would also like to thank a charitable organization: The Friends of the City Churches, whose volunteers ensure that many of our priceless pieces of religious heritage still remain accessible to visitors. The history and heritage of London City is so important and were it not for such caring organizations, more and more church doors might become almost permanently locked.

www.london-city-churches.org.uk